# "To My Memory Sing"

To Sylvia and Morris

To Wonderful memories

*Rosalind B. Clarkin*

1997

# "To My

# Memory Sing

*A Memoir based on letters and poems from*
*Sol Chick Chaikin*
*An American Soldier in China-Burma-India*
*during World War II*

## ROSALIND BRYON CHAIKIN

Library Research Associates Inc.
Monroe, N.Y.
1997

Library Research Associates, Inc.
474 Dunderberg Road
Monroe, New York 10950

Permissions to reprint:
(1) 18 headlines from the *New York Times:*
    Copyright © by the New York Times Co. Reprinted by Permission
(2) Maps reprinted from *It Began at Imphal:*
    *The Combat Cargo Story* by John G. Martin
    "China-Burma-India Theatre" page 124
    "Bases of the 2nd Combat Cargo Group 1944-1946" page 222

*Library of Congress Cataloging-in-Publication Data:*
Chaikin, Rosalind Bryon,
    To My Memory Sing: memoir of Sol Chick Chaikin, an American
    soldier in China-Burma-India during World War II / Rosalind Bryon
    Chaikin.
        300p.
    Includes bibliographical references and index.
    ISBN:0-912526-77-7
    1. Chaikin, Sol C.   2. Chaikin, Rosalind Bryon   3. World War,
1939-1945 — United States — Biography.   4. Trade-unions —
United States — Officials and employees — Biography.   I. Title.
    CT275.C44C44      1997
    940.54'8173—dc21                                        96-29627
                                                              CI P

To my children, grandchildren,
great grandchildren
born and yet to be born.

To my beloved Chick
who lives forever in us all.

# Table of Contents

# Introduction

*"...He added to the honor of this age."*
SENATOR DANIEL PATRICK MOYNIHAN

*"...He was an incurable romantic. We all grew up in the house believing in love."*
ROBERT, ERIC, DAVID AND KAREN CHAIKIN

Sol Chick Chaikin was unusual in every way — at once fun-loving and serious, with a keen intellect and an uncanny ability to connect with people and community. From the day we met I was taken with his energy and the way he made a day come alive in simple ways — a well told story, a burst of song, his ever present broad and glorious smile — and then, of course, the impromptu poems.

Chick and I met in 1938 when I was 15 and he was 20. We were married in 1940, separated for 14 months by his army service in World War II, and until Chick's death, in 1991, we lived unconventional lives in thought and deeds, even as we were enriched by the traditional values of children, family, friends and work.

His Russian immigrant parents expected him to become a successful attorney. But growing up in the 1930's, Chick was ignited by the Roosevelt victory and the emerging New Deal policies. He understood that new labor laws meant new opportunities for working people. After graduating from Brooklyn Law School, he chose to organize workers.

He rose through the ranks from organizer to President of the International Ladies' Garment Workers' Union (ILGWU), Vice President of the AFL-CIO, and became an internationally known labor leader. He energized everyone around him. People responded to his passion and intellectual insights, to his drive toward solutions that could lead to a better life for hard-working, poorly-paid people. Stuart Eizenstat, Assistant to President Carter in domestic affairs said, "...no one was a more articulate advocate for the right of working people to live in dignity." At the 1980 Democratic Convention Chick seconded the nomination of President Jimmy Carter — the first labor leader ever given that honor.

Over the years Chick became a much sought after speaker to an unusually diverse audience —from union meetings and political rallies to international conferences, academic seminars, and top government groups here and abroad. When Chick spoke, people listened. Always impeccably dressed and perfectly groomed, he could speak with conviction and compassion for twenty minutes, one hour, two hours or more, using only a few scrawled notes. He kept his audience spellbound throughout. His strong irrepressible voice was heard defending human rights everywhere, promoting better health and education for all citizens, urging a dialogue among labor, government, and business leaders for a rational trade policy. Mario Cuomo, who credited Chick with giving him the critical support he needed in his first gubernatorial race in New York, said, "He worked hard to get the rest of us to remember those that the world is always more comfortable forgetting."

Reporters enjoyed interviewing him, and he relished the give-and-take. Always hoping to get a good story, they were never disappointed. His answers were to the point, diplomatic, without jargon, always quotable — he could think on his feet. When an interview ended, I never heard him say, "I should have said…"

Chick's wide community interests led him to serve on hospital, university and many other non-profit boards. He became a strong advocate for planning and building the Jacob Javits Convention Center in New York City, and was elected chairman of the board. In 1989, retired from the union, he was designated President and CEO. It was his last job.

Writing came easily to Chick, but he refused to spend his time that way. Instead, he loved speaking to an audience, any audience — one person or thousands. Since he was often asked for a copy of his speech, I suggested he have them taped and transcribed. Because of his gift for cutting to the heart of an issue, the speeches are a powerful collection of essays on many current economic issues. They were subsequently assembled into a book entitled A Labor Viewpoint:

Another Opinion (1980, Library Research Associates Inc.). It was well reviewed.

Though Chick was enormously pleased with the result and referred to the volume often, he still refused to do serious writing. He would say, "It's too pretentious, Ros; I'm not a scholar nor an academician. I exhort, persuade, provoke, even intimidate here and there. Mostly I implore — and I'm good at that. I'm not a writer." The letters here belie those words. He could analyze a problem so that lay people, as well as scholars, could understand the complexities. Much of the cadence of his written language is narrative poetry. Federal Judge Jack B. Weinstein said, "Chick wore words like brilliant jewels."

Within this impressive public figure lived the man, my husband. Equally passionate in our personal life, Chick had the heart of a romantic and the soul of a poet. He could be content for days, even weeks, just the two of us — reading, thinking, talking, allowing his mind to float free with no need to move, go or do.

Although he could spin wonderful tales pinpointing the essence of an incident — a worker's plight, an employer's plaint, a Senator's hearing, a prime minister's mien, Chick shared very few stories about his army years, and only bits and pieces about his fourteen months overseas. After his army service, ending in 1946, he made no attempt to meet with army friends nor participate in reunions. He put the painful army years behind him and did not look back until one evening in March of 1991.

Chick and I were watching video reports of the Persian Gulf War, featuring young soldiers in the desert being interviewed by reporters. The scenes unleashed a torrent of tears neither of us could control, along with memories we thought were forgotten. He turned to me and asked if I still had his letters from World War II. Packed in a large straw picnic basket, buried somewhere in the furthest corner of the basement, we had not looked at them for more than forty years. What would we find, I wondered, and what memories would they evoke? I promised to ferret them out.

There was no time to do that. Chick died of heart failure on April 1, 1991.

After his death I searched for the letters and discovered a treasure.

I want our children and grandchildren to hear his remarkable voice as a young man, to know him in his own language of love, wit and intelligence — to feel his indomitable spirit.

This memoir is the collection of letters and poems from our courtship and army days. They are but moments in our life, yet expressive of the lives of so many young people who find themselves torn apart for a time because of war, work or family stress.

It is our story, a peek into a personal, emotional heart.

Rosalind Bryon Chaikin

# *Prologue*                           1938-1942

*1938 Rosalind Bryon - age 15 - high school graduate.*

*1938  Sol Chick Chaikin - age 20 - law  student*

The New York Times
Feb. 21, 1938, March 12, 1938
*Courtesy of The New York Times Co.*

Chapter 1

# MY MOTHER'S AMERICAN DREAM 1938

The date for the senior prom, to be held in May 1938, had been announced. I was 15 years old, ready to graduate in June, from Walton High, an all-girl's high school in the West Bronx. I felt awkward and foolish with the precocious and stand-offish 17- and 18-year old boys and girls I'd meet at a dance or social club. On the other hand, boys my own age were silly and giggly around girls and generally uninteresting. I would not invite any of them to my prom. I decided not to go.

My mother, however, had other plans. "Of course, you'll go to your prom," she said. "Everybody goes. It's fun and you'll enjoy it." My immigrant Ma, was in love with everything American. She loved eating out. A cafeteria, the Automat or the local deli were all we could afford, but she always worked it into her budget at least two or three times a month. She loved the movies. A prom was Fred Astaire and Ginger Rogers dancing. It was part of a dream she could not have herself, but why shouldn't I have it? "Ask any nice boy," she'd say. "Just go and have a good time."

She didn't want to understand my reticence. In my mind "any nice boy" could be a terrible bore or worse. "I'm not going," I said. "Please don't bother me."

Several days later, when I arrived home from school, my mother greeted me with, "Rosalind, come walk with me. I'm going to see Beckie. Please keep me company — we won't stay long."

In Russia, Beckie and her husband Sam Chaikin, had been my father's childhood friends. They had renewed their friendship when they discovered how close-by they lived. They had a son I had never met named Sol, whom I knew to be 20 years old and graduating from college. Too old to trigger my interest.

Since my mother and I often walked together, her request was not unusual. 1938 was the depth of the depression, a time when the constitutional had become the best outdoor sport, as well as an opportunity to break free of our one-bedroom apartment, see friends, and all at no expense. Moreover, my mother was still coming out of a deep depression following the shock of my sister's death only three years before (in 1935), from a disease we had never heard of —meningitis. Though still withdrawn myself, I had recovered more and was happy to see her initiating a visit.

The Chaikins too, had suffered the loss of a child (in 1929) when their 4-year old son, without warning, ran into the street and was killed by a car. It was a bittersweet renewal, this friendship bonded by tragedy. My mother spoke of it as we walked. How brave Beckie was to have had another child, Eli, who was now three years old. My mother said she would not do that, because she was too terrified of the responsibilities of caring for children.

We arrived unannounced. Phones were a luxury and neither family could afford one. People simply dropped in. Beckie was delighted and Eli greeted us with smiles and hugs before running off to play. We sat around the kitchen table while she set the tea kettle to boil. Just as she proudly remarked that Sol was starting law school, he burst into the house. Eli welcomed him gleefully and they roughhoused playfully. After the introductions he said, "Call me Chick, everyone else does, except Mom," and headed for the refrigerator to find a treat.

He was tall, nearly six feet, slim and well built, attractive and friendly. His dark wavy hair was combed back neatly. His even features, large enough and small enough, seemed in place in his slender longish face. Strong full eyebrows framed his almond shaped eyes, and when he smiled, crinkly lines appeared at his eyes and his cheeks furrowed. It gave his face an open, welcoming look. Unusual was the word that came to my mind. Good looking, yes — but different. I remember thinking, you couldn't put that face into any category. It was unique and that smile moved you to smile back.

His mother interrupted his refrigerator search and said, "Sol, why don't you take Rosalind to the living room and talk with her while Zina (my mother) and I visit a little?"

Disaster, I thought. What would we say to each other? I was thinking of asking him about the nickname when he said, "Graduating from high school? — Let me show you my high school year book."

Just as I found a seat, he deftly whipped his copy of the Townsend Harris Crimson and Gold year book off the shelf. Not only was this the most prestigious boys' public high school in New York City, where only the brightest were accepted to complete the four year course in three years, but as he turned the pages, he made certain I would see he was everywhere in those pages. President of his class, his valedictory speech on a separate page topped by his silhouette. He was dubbed "The Rising Sol" and voted the most capable in his class. On succeeding pages he appeared as an athletic leader with varsity honors, a General Organization delegate with senior honors and an executive board member of the Crimson and Gold, as well as its business manager. The message was clear. Here was a very bright, very intelligent, very capable person. I was amused at what seemed to me to be his total self absorption. He did most of the talking and showed not the smallest interest in me. I said little and believed he did not care about anything I might say or do. I was a kid — why should he?

I was grateful when my mother came in to say we had to leave. He had come to the end of the book and though I was impressed by his achievements, I was puzzled by his inability to change the subject away from himself.

On the way home my mother asked what I thought of Chick. "He only talked about himself," I said.

"He seemed very nice and friendly, and I think he is smart."

I agreed with that but shrugged off her comments with, "I'm sure he's probably very nice," and promptly put him out of my mind.

Over the next several weeks the school was abuzz with preparations for the senior prom to be held in May. I remained disinterested. My mother, however, came alive.

"What! Not go to your prom! Of course, you're going. You must go." I ignored her comments until the nagging became intolerable. There was no respite in the 3-room apartment, nowhere to hide.

After weeks of her stubborn pestering, I shouted at her, "I may have to go to school, but I do not have to go to my prom."

In the most plaintive and serious voice she said, "If you don't go to your prom, you'll regret it the rest of your life."

Where had her sanity gone? It was her American dream and only I could live it for her. I sat quietly for a few minutes to calm down and think. After my anger abated, I said, "I don't know anyone I would ask and besides, we can't afford a gown."

"Ask Sol," she said. "He's a nice boy and I'll make you a beautiful gown." She was a skilled dressmaker.

It was the most ludicrous idea imaginable. Of course, he would never go, but I saw the perfect way to silence her. Luckily, neither Chick nor I had a phone, so I would write him a letter. He would say how nice, but sorry, he just couldn't make it and that would be that. Relieved, I touched my mother gently. "He won't accept," I said. "He's 20 and I'm 15; it just isn't possible."

She said, "nonsense, of course he'll accept. You're a nice girl — smart and beautiful. It's a prom, why wouldn't he go?"

Embarrassed but resigned, I sat down and quickly scribbled an invitation. One week later his answer arrived.

❖

Feb. 24, 1938

My Dear Rosalind:

I was agreeably surprised to hear from you, and I trust that the reply to your letter finds your family and yourself in the best of health.

However, I was disappointed at the brevity of your letter, for I imagine that, once you did begin to write, you should have taken full advantage of your opportunity. Certainly, I should have enjoyed it perhaps more than you would (it's so easy to read, so hard to write).

Be that as it may, let us turn to the business at hand (as one of my Law profs is wont to say). I should be grateful for the chance to escort you to your Prom. And I am! But why you ask a person as boring and ordinary as I am, shall forever remain a mystery to me! I am half tempted to give you a chance to change your mind, but I won't! Young Lady, I accept!

You may recall, however, that you forgot to mention the date of the dance. I hope I don't have the misfortune of having an exam the day after, or so. Now won't you let me know just when the Prom will take place, so that my fears may be allayed?

I should like to pay you a visit soon, but I'm very busy these days: yet I will get around to it; I promise. On second thought, why don't you come around.

Regards,
CHICK

Audubon 3-8514

# The 1938 Microcosm
### College of the City of New York
### 139th Street and Convent Avenue

HOWARD A. KIEVAL
Editor-in-Chief

SOLOMON S. CHAIKIN
Managing Director

IRVING I. ANDERMA!
Business Manage

Feb. 24, 1938

My Dear Rosalind:

I was agreeably surprised to hear from you; and I trust that the reply to your letter finds your family and yourself in the best of health.

However, I was disappointed at the brevity of your letter, for I imagine, that, once you did begin to write, you should have taken full advantage of your opportunity. Certainly, I should have enjoyed it, perhaps more than you would (it's so easy to read, so hard to write!).

Be that as it may, let us turn to the business at hand (as one of my Law Profs is wont to say). I should be grateful for the chance to escort you to your Prom. And I am! But why you ask a person as boring and ordinary as I am, shall forever remain a mystery to me! I am half tempted to give you a chance to change your mind, but I won't! Young Lady, I accept!

You may recall, however, that you forgot to to mention the date of the Dance. I hope I don't have the misfortune of having an exam the day after, or so. how won't you let me know just when the Prom will take place, so that my fears may be allayed?

I should like to pay you a visit, soon, but I'm very busy these days; yet I will get around to it; I promise. On second thought, why don't you come around

Regards,

Chick

7

The New York Times
Sept. 27, 1938, Sept. 29, 1938
*Courtesy of The New York Times Co.*

Chapter 2

## SHE: BUIDING A FRIENDSHIP

## HE: GETTING HOOKED                  1938-39

My brilliant plan had backfired. How could it? I read and re-read his response trying to unravel the puzzle. I was sure he did not want to go. His words told me that. "But why you ask a person as boring and ordinary as I am " gave it away. These were not the words of the young confident Townsend Harris man I had seen. He was a self-assured person who knew his own worth. Why was he patronizing me, and why did he agree to go?

My mother was no help. She maintained her "I told you so" position and, brushing aside my questions, said, "I don't know what's wrong with you, Rosalind. He wrote you a nice letter. What more do you want?" With that, she turned her attention to make good her promise and work on a gown. Together with a friend, she shopped for fabric and trimmings; they chattered and beamed like two teenagers with bargain purchases. Their excitement was contagious. I began to lose myself in their preparations. I loved the gossamer pink chiffon they found and couldn't wait to see what their nimble fingers would fashion. After only two fittings the dress blossomed into a beautifully tailored creation with a classic, form-fitting waist, heart-shaped neckline, huge puffed sleeves trimmed with hand-made satin bows and finished with a double layered, bias-cut skirt that swayed with the rhythm of my every movement.

At the same time, my emotions zig-zagged between pleasure and despair. The prom was weeks away. I wondered briefly if Chick would write, visit, or call. Although we didn't have phones in our homes, in an emergency my family could be reached by calling a phone number in the basement of our apartment building. The superintendent would answer, come upstairs and we would rush down to talk. Chick's family could be reached by calling the candy store phone located on his street corner. The store owner would send anyone available to deliver the

9

message. A call, like a telegram, usually meant bad news and short of a death in the family, we avoided it. Chick had no reason to call. A letter with a three cent stamp or a penny postcard arrived overnight. But why would he write or even come by? I hardly knew him and I assumed I would not see or hear from him again until the night of the prom. Wary and anxious, still wondering why he had said yes to my invitation, I approached the evening with trepidation, anticipating disaster. All the while I told myself over and over that it was only one evening — I could surely get through one evening. Then life would be back to normal.

My mother's ride on Cloud 9 continued. With the gown ready, she took on the problems of my appearance. "You'll need some make up, some lipstick, and of course I'll curl your hair." I was past arguing. I did insist on buying my own lipstick and accessories, but I would let her expert hands curl my hair.

Then my friend Norma confided in me at school. Her mother had arranged a date for her.

"Do you know him?" I asked.

"No, but my mom says he's a law student," she said. "I don't know anything else about him, but I don't care. At least I'll be going to the prom."

What a stroke of luck! "Oh, Norma, can't we go together?" I pleaded. "It would be perfect — you know, two law students!"

"My mother will set it up." she said. "She's good at that."

I wondered about the difference between us. Why couldn't I think like Norma or my mother, just go and have a good time instead of worrying whether or not "he" is going to enjoy the evening? Well, that was me and it didn't look as if I was going to change. Double dating would make it easier.

I loved dressing up for the prom. I tried to keep calm as the butterflies fluttered overtime in my stomach. When I looked in the mirror, I had to admit the makeup made a big difference. I liked my new face, with a frame of softly curled hair looking back at me. My mother made the final inspection and said, "The ugly duckling has become a swan."

The bell rang, my mother opened the door and Chick entered carrying a corsage of deep pink sweetheart roses, the perfect choice.

When I turned to look at him, his bright open smile eased my tension and I noticed the hazel of his eyes for the first time.

"You look lovely," he said, pinning the corsage on my left shoulder.

"You look handsome, too," I said.

He beamed, "It's not a rented tux. It's my own, so it fits right." Imagine, his own tuxedo! I guess he likes dressing up too, I thought.

Within minutes Norma and her date Mark arrived to share a cab. The evening was shaping up. I didn't have to worry about conversation now that Chick had someone his own age to talk with. The last of my anxiety dissolved as soon as we arrived at the gym.

With the opening beat of the band, Chick quickly moved us onto the open floor. How he could dance! A strong leader, his movements smooth and on beat, he could Fox Trot, Peabody, Waltz, Rumba, Tango — and I could follow. He responded to the rhythms gracefully and I to his lead. As we danced, our conversation was easy.

"You seem so comfortable in formal clothes," I said. "Most guys complain about stiff collared shirts."

"Not me, I don't mind starched collars at all. I wear them whenever I go out. I like the way they look."

"You must date many girls."

He laughed. "No, usually just one at a time, but I recently broke off with someone I've known for two years."

"Why, what happened?"

"She wanted to become engaged. I'm not ready for that. I've just started law school and I have too many things to do and think about first. I decided I'm off women for a while."

I didn't take his comment personally since I was sure tonight's date was an obligation. I understood his feelings perfectly — at 15, I was nowhere ready to think about a steady boy friend, much less an engagement or marriage.

The music carried us along. He would sing with the band a few measures of a favorite song as he whirled me about the floor. With his easy and confident manner I felt warm and happy. And so it was, in small subtle steps, the evening was transformed.

It no longer mattered why he had accepted my invitation. What counted was this bright, sophisticated, handsome, young law student

11

enjoying the evening with me. When Chick escorted me home, there was no goodnight peck on the cheek or clumsy try for a kiss; instead, he invited me to his June dance. A perfect evening.

My mother greeted me with, "He fell in love with you Rosalind, the moment he saw you." I did not believe that, and waved her comment aside. I kissed her. "You were so right about the prom. It was fun. We all had a super good time."[1]

I assumed he would move on to date others after the June dance, but he didn't. It was so easy for him to take a break mid-week from the routine of study and law school, walk over to our house unannounced and visit. We were always prepared for spontaneous visits from friends with coffee, tea, milk, homemade cookies, doughnuts and other treats. From June 1938 through January 1939, we dated, at first occasionally, then every week.

On balmy nights, we would take long walks around the reservoir nearby about a three mile hike. We talked and talked and talked of what my future and his might be. Prospects were not bright for lawyers graduating without connections. He could expect to earn eight to ten dollars a week in some small firm practicing law of little interest to him. He was becoming disenchanted with that choice. I started college in September of 1938 without a specific direction. The world scene was grim. Hitler was a serious threat; we were alarmed about his book Mein Kampf, worried about its contents of "German Uber Alles" and the anti-Semitic threats. We talked about the reactionary Father Coughlin in this country, a leader of the America First movement, with whose isolationist philosophy we did not agree. Chick was violently anti-Communist as well as anti-Fascist. We were never at a loss for things to talk about.

On occasion, he would come bouncing in early on Saturday morning, yank me out of a late morning sleep to walk with him to the library for study, reading, talking, laughing and listening. Soon we graduated to a movie and soda. When his friend could borrow his father's car, we'd savor a treat — dancing, dancing, dancing at

---

1    Chick wrote of this evening in his poem *My Odyssey Page* 178

Schmidts Farm in Westchester, which cost four dollars. We pooled our money. Chick borrowed two dollars from me on Saturday night and paid it back on the Wednesday visit.

I had a few dates with other boys. All hands and groping fingers converted an evening into evasion tactics — no fun. Chick kept distance between us. He still wanted to be free and uninvolved. I looked forward to our times together. They were always fun and not ever predictable. He never made a pass. I didn't expect him to; after all, he was (now) 21 and I was 16. We had built a friendship.

By January 1939, Chick felt completely at home in our apartment. From time to time, on the Wednesday visits, he would reach for paper and pencil and toss off a poem.

❖

## ODE TO A PICKUP

So lovely you are
That the stars up above
Pale and grow dimmer
When you appear, my love

Such beauty as this
Is only found in such place
As where the rose whose scent
Sweetens the air of the desert space.

Such form as is yours
Well puts Venus to shame
All this I know, but
What's your name!

13

## ODE TO THE MARCH WIND!

Blow wind blow on my lady fair
You disrupt her attire, tousle her hair
Bring blushes of red to her white cheek
Blow wind blow, what if houses creak

When your mighty breath in a lion's roar
Rattles the windows and slams the door
What care I if you blow all day
So long as you don't blow my love away!

❖

     Between visits he would send a note, even when he had little to say. How else to keep in touch without phones?

❖

Tues nite

Dear Rosalind,

I have only just put my books aside and in as much as I have little thought of sleep, I take paper from the closet and pencil from vest pocket and prepare to spend some pleasant moments with you.

Somehow, at the present time, with little thought of sleep or study or other responsibility, I seem to share, if only momentarily, your feeling of freedom. It is the sort of feeling that wants me to get up and about. But at this late hour, there is little one can do, that is, do well or satisfactorily.

So while night finds me safely ensconced in an easy chair near the radio the only pleasure I can get from the fleeting and newly acquired "liberty" must come thinking of what you have been doing with your time. I have no doubt you are doing all that can possibly be done to make these "free days" chuck full of enjoyment and pleasantries.

So be it - you have earned it.

Now I hear voices asking to put the lights out, and retire. That this request should have come so early and at a time when this letter had only just begun is surely to be regretted, by me at least, for these visits with you are certainly welcome

I shall, I hope, see you Fri. Nite.

Until then — Go To The Movies,
And Enjoy Yourself
— CHICK —

15

## FRUSTRATION,
## (OR WHY DO THESE THINGS HAPPEN TO ME?)

I leaped to my charger
Prancing in wait
And spurred him on
And increased his gait.

Thru meadow and field
Thru forest and town
Dodging all pitfalls and shouting
Make way for the courier of the crown.

Night after night as we sped along
My horse never tiring and with little rest
We arrived one day at the castle of the lord
Who welcomed me and said we served him best.

And then the lord, to show his gratitude
Asked my wish and as I started to beam
And began to ask for you,
I slipped and awoke from my dream

❖

The few letters and youthful poems that are interspersed here reveal the courting game, the reaching out and pulling back, the stirrings he felt, needing more emotionally while wanting to stay uninvolved intellectually.

❖

Thursday PM

*ROSALIND—

Surprising it is, that in the midst of a famous Supreme Court decision concerning abrogation of the "gold clauses" from private individual contract (see Norman vs Baltimore and Ohio RR) that my thought should turn to you. Surprising yes, but logical too, for when one's mind is weary of names, places, dates, and logical reasoning, isn't it the subconscious that always interjects itself into your orderly processes and forces your mind into a consideration of more pleasant thoughts — of mice, men and lovely young ladies? And the one thing that isn't so surprising, the one thing I am truly grateful of is that I may number you to be among the class of "lovely young ladies," who I am sure it is a privilege to know. And as if to give proof to that prophet of old who said with such eminent wisdom, "All things come to pass," I do know you!

And even as I write these lines, comes the thought that I should like still more for us to become better acquainted. Yet, as if to spite my very wish, the time that might well be spent in furthering this design, must needs be spent, poring over books, remembering by rote, names, places, dates, and old legal decisions.

Much as I regret my inability to pay you a much longed for visit, I still persist in turning the pages of a remarkably dry volume! For isn't it true, that even the squirrel must labor thru the summer, so that his winter may find him well fed and comfortable! Only then may he raise his voice and heart in happy song, and sing, "Tis the season to be jolly."

And so with us! In order that we may face our free moments with that selfsame spirit, must we not now labor and deny ourselves fleeting pleasures?

All of which should imply by now that I'm studying hard and that I miss you! I miss your smiling face, the walks we took, the things we talked about — and also, those doughnuts — I hope too, that you are taking advantage of my enforced absence and that you too are "swatting the books".

It is my hope that you do well — Somehow I know that you will. And if it will help any, you may know, that I'm pulling for you" — Go to it!! I have to get back to the grind; this visit with you has been more than refreshing —

Good-bye and good Luck.

Regards to the folks
Love, CHICK

*My Dear Roslyn


## FIRST IMPRESSIONS　　　　　　　　Jan 1939

I tip my hat to gentlemen
When ladies fall, they stay that way
I put salt in my coffee, pepper in tea
Funny how I act since we met that day

Tues. PM

Dear Rosalind,

Well here it is the first day A.E. — after exams — alive and kicking, but not much of either. Really, at the present time, (just finished some studying — vacation's over) I don't feel much like anything. Indifferent I guess — I thought earlier this evening that I might walk over to your place, but I fell asleep and was up too late — studied and it was then much later — hence no walk — but then the next best thing was this letter.

I was downtown this afternoon and got some tickets for Rocket to the Moon. I hope you haven't seen that.** The tickets are for Mon. Feb. 13th (holiday) matinee. If you can make it, we"ll make a day of it downtown.

I couldn't get tickets for what I like for Sat nite, as yet. But I'm going to try again Wed or Thurs.

Whatever happens though — We'll have some fun at that — You know since I began this letter, I've developed a yearning for a good long walk — Couldn't you come over to my place Thurs nite at about 7:30 and then we'll walk our feet off — weather permitting. I understand tho that it is going to be clear and cold — "Weather Man" is a pal of mine, and he guarantees not to cross me up.

So why not try hard, and come over — if you can.

If you're not over then by 8:00 — I'll just fold up and grieve — and that's not pleasant is it. Until then—

Regards to the folks

CHICK

**2 to 1 you have though —

19

## OPUS XXIVCCMVII

The cries of strong men rent the air
With shouts of defiance 'gainst the foe
Whose hosts it seemed were everywhere
Outnumbering our heroes who gave blow for blow.

A sad day it seemed was at hand
For the defenders of truth and right
As their attackers rushed on our little band
And the din of battle was heard in the night

All seemed lost as dawn came thru
And the sun heralded a newborn day
When suddenly a shout, and I knew
That it meant you joined in the fray.

You, great men of old
Who could not sit by
And see men so brave and bold
Go down before the foe and die.

You could not bear to see
That which you have fought in the past,
Conquer and subjugate so terribly
The truth and right that should always last Forever!

Bewildered was I, with mind in a daze
I started to speak, but to no avail
I couldn't find the reason why
My entire life upset or senses fail.
But suddenly it came to me
That you were standing by
And saying that you were in love
With a certain someone close by.


## YOUNG MAN'S FATE

Study, study rack your brain
If any there be, put it to work
Page after page, read them again
Come now, be sure, don't try to shirk

For exam and exam are coming along
So prepare for them now while you have the chance
For time is short but it won't be long
Till you're again taking your sweetheart out to the dance.


❖


    Looking back, I can see how he baited the hook. Naive as I was, I never saw myself in these early poems and remained unaware of his growing dilemma.


❖

The New York Times
April 29, 1939, Aug.1939, Sept. 1, 1939, Sept. 3, 1939, Sept. 17, 1939
*Courtesy of The New York Times Co.*

Chapter 3

# EVERYTHING CHANGES 1939

By late January 1939, we had been seeing each other for about nine months. The country was in a deep depression and we recognized how lucky we were to be able to attend college. There were several free New York city colleges; Chick had attended the College of the City of New York (CCNY), the all-boys school, and I was now enrolled at Hunter College for girls in Manhattan.

These excellent schools offered higher education for very little money to thousands of qualified students. At first I received my books free, but in spite of protest from the students, the school began charging a three-dollar book fee for each semester. A science lab meant an additional three dollars. All students lived at home and commuted to school. I had no problems with my two-dollar-a-week allowance. It paid for my carfare (ten cents a day) and lunch (twenty-five cents a day) and left me fifty cents a week for a movie or treat.

There was no doubt about my commitment to college. There was so much to learn — I wanted that — and I would receive the first degree in my family. It could lead to a better job, better pay, and a more interesting life. It was a dream come true for every Jewish immigrant family in our circle. I would not waste this opportunity, and when work became available, I wanted to be ready.

My mother urged me to take the business major. It was practical and she thought an office job was ideal. I resisted. My major interest was science. Although I knew we could not afford the cost of a medical career, I decided to major in physiology and chose a psychology minor. To my mother's query, "What will you do with that?" I replied, "I'll become a dietitian or something."

In fact, I did not know what kind of work I would find, but I was fascinated by the sciences and particularly with the study of the human body. I wanted to learn everything on the subject in the four years ahead. But since I would need to work, I included courses in elementary school education as a fall back position, and hoped for the best when I'd graduate in 1942.

One Saturday night as we strolled around the reservoir, Chick began to talk about some decisions he had made. "I've been giving some serious thought to my future," he said, "and I decided that law is not for me."

"Why not?"

"I just can't see myself chasing an ambulance to pick up a client, or representing someone who wants to sue the city about a crack in the sidewalk, or buried in research and writing briefs. That's not for me."

"Your parents will be so disappointed," I said. "What about school?"

"Oh, I'll finish law school and take the bar." he said, "I'm more than halfway there now."

He enjoyed the classes and knew that everything he learned would be useful, no matter what he did.

"A degree is an asset," he said, "and my folks will accept what I do easier."

From many earlier conversations I already knew that Chick was interested in the union movement and how it could help working people. He often argued that people should have something to say about their pay and working conditions. I remembered his stories of listening to his father in the 1930's, argue and debate with his working buddies about the problems they faced in their factory. Sam was an active member of the International Ladies' Garment Workers' Union (ILGWU), in an industry that Chick knew, understood and loved. Even then, Chick saw many opportunities for workers emerging from the Roosevelt New Deal labor policies. It seemed to me these interests could easily be combined with his legal background.

"You could always be a labor lawyer."

"No, I don't want that. These are exciting times, Ros. It's illegal for a boss to interfere with organizing — and you know — workers don't know their rights. They need a leader. That's for me!"

I admired his desire to be where the action was and said so.

"I don't kid myself," he said. "It won't be easy." Then nodding his head, he said, "I'd like to be an organizer for the ILG. It's what I want to do. Besides, I know a lot about that industry."

We were now on the last lap of our walk. Chick had become quiet, deep in his own thoughts. As we passed a park bench he stopped, and suggested we rest for a while, something we rarely did. He sat looking straight ahead, not at me, seemingly lost in thought. Then, turning to face me, he said, "Ros, I won't be coming by anymore. Things are getting too serious between us and I'm not ready for that. It'll be best if I don't come again."

Stunned and speechless, I thought, "What happened? Did I miss something here? How could a friendship be 'too serious?' All we do is walk, talk, laugh, dance and enjoy. We hardly even hold hands." When I could bring myself to speak, I didn't try to dissuade him. I just said, "I don't understand the problem, but it's your choice."

He said nothing more, just nodded his head pensively, and we got up to go. He walked me home and said goodnight. When he left, I felt abandoned. My head was spinning, my thoughts jumping from this to that. So many strange feelings surfaced. I would miss him so much — the talks, the fun, the conversations, the dancing. But just being near was important. We had never talked of love or of a future together. Was this love? There were too many obstacles to even think of love and marriage, and this was certainly the worst time to think of it at all. There were years of school ahead for me, jobs were scarce — how could we support ourselves? I always assumed he needed someone older, more sophisticated, less naive. That was it, I decided. He was not dating anyone else, I was sure of that. He was right. It had to end. Now was the best time. But did it really mean he would never come by to visit again? I felt an emptiness I had never known before. Nothing made sense.

My mother and father had been prodding me to date other boys. They both thought I was too young for a steady boy-friend and kept suggesting I try to reach out more. Well, I thought, they won't be unhappy when Chick doesn't come by next week. I just couldn't think of dating anyone at this time and decided to say nothing to either of them until I could sort things out better myself.

On Wednesday, my parents were in the living room listening to the radio. Despondent and subdued, I turned to a demanding assignment, hoping to keep my mind occupied. Restless, I still could not focus. I kept pushing myself to get going when the bell rang.

Wondering who it could be, I opened the door. There he stood, smiling, relaxed, as though this was just the usual visit. My puzzled expression quickly changed. His eyes connected with mine and came alive with glints of pleasure that needed no words. Unlike Saturday night, when he was debating what to do, looking ahead, and confronting problems, tonight he seemed carefree, every movement upbeat.

With my parents in the room, I did not question his arrival or probe for an explanation. Besides, our body language said it all. He couldn't stay away, and I was delighted to see him back. I expected that sometime in the course of the evening, he would explain his change of heart.

We chatted as though nothing had happened, and then he reached for the yellow lined pad on the table, as he had on other visits, and wrote LOVE IS GONE — a poem so beautiful and moving, telling me much of the inner turmoil he could not speak.

❖

## LOVE IS GONE

Desolate —
As a sandy beach bearing no human print.
Lonely —
As one who has labored and at the end of his stint
Can find nothing more to engage his mind

Discontented —
As the wind which sweeps down the mountain tops
Restless —Ruthless, crushing every thing until it stops
And searches everywhere a fitting grave to find.

So am I —
Sorrowing now that my love has left
Without me —
Leaving me so unnerved, grieving, bereft
Searching ever for friendship, or love or peace of mind!

❖

After my parents said goodnight and retired for the night, I started to ask what the poem meant. Who was his lost love and what about Saturday when he said...

He reached out to me, embraced me and held me close, kissed me long and lovingly; I kissed him back and everything changed.

*Rosalind  1939*

The New York Times
April 19, 1940, May10-18-30, 1940
*Courtesy of The New York Times Co.*

The New York Times
June 11-15- 23, 1940, Sept. 4-11. 1940
*Courtesy of The New York Times Co.*

*Meyer & Zina Bryon*    *Rosalind and Chick*

*Beckie, Eli and Sam Chaikin*

Chapter 4

# ALL THE OBSTACLES ARE OVERCOME  1939-1941

By June of 1940, Chick and I were dating seriously. During that month he graduated from St. Lawrence Brooklyn Law School, and prepared to take his Bar exam. The evening before the exam, instead of the last minute studying most law students engaged in, he came to visit. At my questioning glance, he waved his hand and said, "It'll be a breeze. I know everything I need to know. I'm not concerned." He snuggled up close and said, "this is a perfect time to listen to some music and relax with you for awhile."

It was a warm and happy evening and when he was ready to leave I said, "Good luck tomorrow."

His look of utter disdain caught me by surprise. He said, "I don't need luck."

How extraordinary, I thought, how unlike me. He always knew, without hesitation what he could do and what he wanted, while I questioned if I would accomplish what I set out to do, and juggled choices.

Chick finished his Bar exam in half the allotted time and was certain he had passed. Then, just as he had already decided, he speedily put the practice of law behind him and proceeded to follow through on his decision to become an organizer.

In the one year that had passed, from 1939 to 1940, a new and frightening word had become part of the American lexicon — Blitzkrieg — a German word that translates to Lightning War.

By 1939 Hitler had already taken Austria and Czechoslovakia. In September of 1939 he marched into Poland, England, and France declared war. In the same month, The Soviet Union signed a ten-year non-aggression pact with Hitler, sending the American communists scurrying to explain this treachery.

With the removal of any threat from the Russian Bear on the east, Hitler was free to continue his assault against an essentially demilitarized Europe. With unprecedented speed he proceeded to overrun Denmark, Norway, Holland, Belgium, and Luxembourg. In June of 1940, Italy joined the German axis and Hitler took Paris. France fell and England was under siege with rockets and nightly air raids.

Though the war news was terrifying, Chick and I did not believe it would come to our shores. We still felt protected by our two oceans, but we were in real distress about the predominantly isolationist point of view in the country. How could a democratic country survive in a Fascist world? We argued for doing everything we could to help the European democracies. Chick and I agreed the country should build an army and prepare a strong military defense program. We believed a peacetime draft was inevitable.

Roosevelt pressed to support the allied effort by trading destroyers (that Great Britain needed desperately) for sea bases, and later on, creating a lend-lease scheme for materiel. Congress fought to remain neutral, and some Republicans threatened impeachment.

Among our friends, what to do and how to do it was endless fodder for discussion and argument, with Chick leading the tirade against the Russians for removing themselves from the fight.

But though we were concerned about the war, it did not interfere with our daily lives. The summer months of 1939 and 1940 are priceless memories. Except for rainy nights, we spent every evening in July and August at the famous City College outdoor Lewisohn stadium in Manhattan. The college leased the sports center each summer for unusual cultural events, where only the most outstanding performers appeared for concerts, operas, and ballets. Chick was lucky to have a job selling soft drinks, beer, and ice-cream at a stand there. Since he could only sell before a performance and during intermission, we could sit and enjoy the evening together. Seats were 25 cents, 50 cents, or $1.00 each, but even the cheapest seats, plus carfare, were too much to add to our weekly expenses. Chick, who knew the ticket taker at the dollar gate, arranged to have him let me in free of charge. What a treat!

Once inside the stadium, the sounds of musicians tuning up mingled with the hubbub of people greeting one another, and the sprinkle of laughter here and there set the stage for another happy evening where people came, ready to let go and have a good time. I would skirt around the comfortable padded folding chairs that were set-up for the performance on the grounds of the stadium, and head for the 50 cent section where Chick had his stand. There I would catch the shouts of young men hawking their wares. "Soda, beer, get your ice-cold drinks here." Some sold pillows for the tiers of hard white stone seating that made up the rows of the stadium.

Reilly, a small, slender man, whose job it was to prevent anyone from sneaking down to the dollar area, stood at the steps between the sections. For two summers, each time I came by, he would pull himself up to his full height (about five foot seven inches) his arms akimbo, his ruddy face stern, but not in any way intimidating, and he'd say, "Sorry Miss, you can't go up there." And each time I would reply, "No, no, it's O.K. for me to go up, you have to stop them from coming down to the dollar section." he'd think about it for a moment, nod his head, then let me pass. But he was clearly puzzled. Chick had told him to expect me, but he felt he just would not be doing his job right if he didn't stop me. One day toward the end of the second summer, he found the courage to approach Chick, "Your girl friend must be very rich. How come she pays a dollar to go up to the fifty cent section?"

Chick replied, "Don't worry Reilly, it's O.K. she's an heiress."

The evenings were glorious. We heard the brilliant violinist Isaac Stern play with the Philharmonic, listened to the exquisite coloratura soprano Lily Pons, were captivated by the special productions of Aida and Carmen, as well as the performances of the Fokine and Petit Ballets. Each year, the Paul Whiteman orchestra presented a rousing Gershwin program, with Oscar Levant at the piano playing the Rhapsody in Blue. Enveloped in the musical wonders of Bach, Beethoven, Brahms, Mozart and more, Chick's arms held me close, as the sky slipped into twilight, and the stars emerged speckling the cobalt blue sky.

After the performance, Chick stacked new cans of soda into the cooler, buried them under buckets of ice, and closed off the stand for the next night's performance. At about 11:00 PM, we headed back to the Bronx on the subway and arrived home about midnight. Once in a while, after he left my apartment, he would stand across the street and break into song — usually singing a melody from the night's concert. I would hear his strong baritone voice, run to open my window, laugh and wave until he'd start his 15-minute walk home. Some neighbors were roused as well, but they never complained. I loved those nights, and I loved Chick.

It was during one of those days in August of 1940, that Chick was interviewed by the President of the ILGWU, David Dubinsky, for an organizing job. On the same day he received news that he passed the Bar, he also learned he was hired by the ILG for the grand salary of twenty dollars a week ($1040 a year). He was to start organizing in Fall River, Massachusetts.

Rushing over to share the good news, we stared at each other and broke into laughter. Suddenly all the obstacles were overcome. We could live adequately on his salary and we were deeply in love. We chose to reach for some happiness in spite of the uncertainty of what another year of Hitler's madness might bring.

Chick said, "We can be married in two weeks." He did not need to ask.

Chick was twenty-two, but since I was seventeen, I would need my parent's consent. Then, only a judge could marry us in New York State.

Our parents were aghast. Each in turn attempted to dissuade us — we were too young, certainly too foolish, and bent on ruining our lives.

My mother asked, "What about school?" I explained that I wanted very much to graduate but since I could not afford anything but a free College, I would finish if she would permit me to continue to live with them. With that promise, my parents relinquished the fight, but not without a final word from my mother. "All I wanted was for you to go to the Prom," she said, "You don't have to marry him!" I shrugged my shoulders and laughed.

"But, I want to make you a wedding," she said. "You are my only child and I've been saving to do that. Besides, it's no marriage without a Rabbi." I loved the idea of a wedding, but I knew my mother would use the preparations to delay the event. It might take her six months to a year to work it all out.

"That's wonderful," I said, "but Chick and I will get married in two weeks by a Judge. When you get it all together, we"ll have the wedding." She was surprised by my new found independence but it convinced her that I was serious. Without any more haggling, my parents accepted the arrangement.

Chick's parents were reeling from the double blow. "Giving up the law to organize? I don't believe it," his father said. And getting married so young?"

But Chick did not discuss it. He simply said, "Yes, that's it."

"Well, at least there'll be a wedding," his father added. "I'll be able to face my friends."

Both sets of parents agreed they would not attend the civil wedding. For them the real wedding would come later and they could wait. They decided it was a splendid opportunity to leave town and enjoy the country air. That was a decided plus for us since it meant complete privacy for the first time with a choice between two apartments to boot.

Chick's cousin Larry and my best friend Florence agreed to come along and be our witnesses. We were married on August 31, 1940 in Yonkers, New York by Judge Frank H. Coyne. He took one look at our four very young, happy faces — I can still see his teasing expression as he said playfully, "I'll try to make this as painless as possible." We all broke up.

One month later, we were married again, this time by a rabbi. It was nothing short of a miracle. My mother, who couldn't buy a dress without shopping every store in the city first, made every decision quickly. Chick and I helped her work out the catering arrangements. With her budget of three hundred dollars (all her savings), we found a beautiful Temple where an unusual buffet dinner was held just after a solemn but joyous service. The live band, long formal satin bridal gown, liquor, photographs, flowers and food for 300 friends and family all came in on budget.

The wedding was wonderful in every way. Chick and I had the best time.

Now, determined to finish my college education, I entered my Junior year at Hunter College in New York City while Chick, assigned to the New England territory, was off on organizing campaigns. He was permitted one weekend in two to get home while I continued to live with my parents in their one-bedroom apartment in the Bronx.

*Rosalind Bryon and Chick Chaikin*
*September 29, 1940*
*A wonderful wedding.*

The separation was painful, but we had both made up our minds to fulfill our part of the bargain. A major difference was that Chick and I could now share my pull-out bed in the living room. It was a cramped arrangement but we were young, and happy to have something.

This frugal arrangement left me enough money to install a phone. My mother viewed this extravagance as just another American indulgence. "Who will pay for it after you leave?" she asked. "I'll take it out if you don't want it," I said.

At first we all used it sparingly. The phone seemed distant, impersonal, and it was an expense. We never used more than the calls allowed each month for the lowest rate, and we never spoke more than the three minutes allowed per call. But everyone agreed it was a definite plus. It served very well as a messenger when time did not allow for a letter. Chick would call to let me know where he was and when he was coming, or if I could come to visit him. Our conversations were restrained, but my parents were most accommodating and tried not to hover about when we talked. My mother began to use the phone to call her friends and to enjoy the convenience. People stopped dropping in unannounced. They called first. "That was nice," she said. It did not take much time for her to see the phone as a necessity, not a luxury, and she never mentioned taking it out again.

I spent every school vacation with Chick in New England. The separation never got easier and from time to time Chick would talk about changing his work so that we could be together.

Many letters were exchanged. Only this one remains.

❖

Monday nite
Providence, Rhode Island
(mailed Tues a.m.)

My Dearest Darling Rosalind

How empty everything seems without you: How dismal the dark, how glaring the light. How I keep thinking of you, and how lovely it would be if only you were near. I have already written to you today. But I can't stop thinking and dreaming of you, so that I must write to tell you. I never was bashful to tell of my love and marriage has made me less so. You are life itself to me and my love for you shall endure as long as life itself.

And sometimes, when I seem so matter of fact, you wonder a little, think of my love and be reassured.

I thought, when I first came to F.R. [Fall River], how nice it would be to come back to you. And I remember now and see in my mind's eye, just how you did look that first time I returned to you and my love. And I keep thinking that you will look the same when next we meet. And when we do, I shall hold you again as I did then and tho it shall be still, I shall hear music timed to the beat of our hearts. And I shall be happy once more. Happy to hold you, to see you, and to kiss you. So wait just a little while longer darling. Hell and high water can't keep me from you...you have always had my heart. I shall bring you my soul.

## CHICK

The New York Times
Apr. 26, 1941, June 22, 1941
*Courtesy of The New York Times Co.*

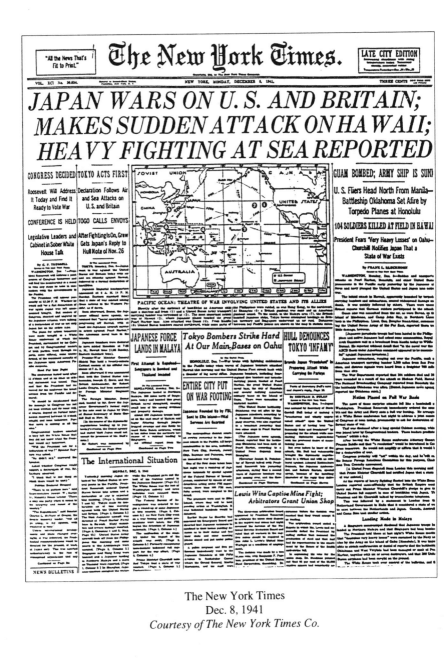

The New York Times
Dec. 8, 1941
*Courtesy of The New York Times Co.*

Chapter 5

## THE UNTHINKABLE HAPPENS                    1941-42

During the exhilarating first weeks on his job, Chick went house to house visiting young women workers and families after their work. He connected quickly and easily with people. They spoke of their fears: They could lose their jobs, be blacklisted at other factories and be out of work for good — all for having joined a union. He could articulate convincingly how unions could help prevent any of that from happening. Now that the law was on their side, they had the right to organize, the right to join a union. Never condescending but speaking simply, he explained the law and encouraged them to join with others to create a majority in the factory so they could vote effectively in secret. They listened and questioned over many evenings and found the courage to take a chance. It wasn't an easy decision. Their dangers were real, and they had to know going in, it could mean a tough battle. More often than not workers, male and female, young and old, responded to the possibility that they could earn more than the 10, 12, or 14 dollars a week they were getting.

He knew he had made the right decision for himself, but we both hated the interminable separation. At times he would think of abandoning his work and trying for another kind of job. Transportation problems compounded his frustration. House to house organizing, on foot or by bus, wasted precious time. Coordinating train schedules for trips back to New York was often impossible.

To solve the problem, we bought a used car. It was a dreamy new red convertible Chevy with extra chrome trim that a young man was forced to give up (at a greatly reduced price) because he'd been drafted. We might have bought an older, cheaper car but we could manage these time payments and who could resist the temptation? We never questioned the value of the purchase.

Because I was still living with my parents, I took some flak about our extravagance. "How could you buy on time?" my mother asked.

"And such a fancy one — you're always looking for trouble!" But just as the telephone had proved its worth, they soon enjoyed the pleasure of being chauffeured about when Chick came home.

We were out driving on December 7, 1941, when screeching static interrupted the radio program and we heard the stunning announcement that Japan had attacked Pearl Harbor. The news sent shock waves through my body. What did it mean? How could this be? The unthinkable had happened. And then I heard Chick saying, "That's it, we're in the fight now — no more hemming and hawing." We rushed home to be in touch with friends and family.

The radio continued to relay news of the devastation the Japanese had inflicted. The country was now plunged irrevocably into war. Wherever we went — friends, parents, relatives — everyone seemed glued to a radio. All we talked about was the war. A major change was taking place. The attack had united the country. The war was now primary, the politics of war was declared bi-partisan, and the all-out effort was to fight and win.

We did not know what it would mean for us. The number of men drafted would surely increase and we would take it as it came. Men, eighteen to twenty-eight years of age, were being called into service. Single men were called first, then married men, then men with one child and so on. Our draft board was not yet looking for married men, but if called, Chick would go, of course. Two of his cousins and several friends were drafted. We knew a few who volunteered, but they were all single men.

Almost from the first day we were married, we talked about starting a family. We agreed we wanted four children, and I hoped to have them before I turned thirty. However, finishing school came first. I had made that commitment. After that, we could find a place of our own and we'd be ready. By February of 1942, Chick would reopen the subject of family from time to time. We didn't have to wait for my graduation in June to start. After all, a baby did take nine months, he would say. The future was always unpredictable. With Chick, I did not fear what lay ahead, nor did I think very much about work. Jobs were still in short supply. The war was only part of the picture, There was Chick's work, which took him from one city to another. Did that matter? Though I did not know where we would live, I was ready to move wherever his work would take us. I agreed with Chick to plan our family, and let life take it course.

I graduated from Hunter College in June of 1942, six months pregnant. When I told my parents, my mother said, "For this you went to college?" A feminist back then, she was frustrated by my lack of ambition for a career. My father was concerned because of the war. "Chick could be called into the army," he said. True, but I did not see it as imminent. I was nineteen.

As the summer of 1942 approached, there were people who believed that German submarines were hovering about our eastern shore and might conceivably land or invade the country. As a result, many of the ocean front summer homes went begging. Chick and I thought the submarine scare was a hoax and dismissed it out-of-hand. Instead, we took advantage of the opportunity to rent a splendid five bedroom home in Gloucester, Massachusetts for an unbelievably low price. Shared with another couple, the cost was negligible.

We enjoyed the luxury of space, the freedom to explore the wonderful beaches and towns nearby, to swim, walk, bask in the pleasure of delicious New England fish and lobsters, union talk, laughter and lots of love. My pregnancy was uneventful, I felt well and happy. It was a memorable summer far removed from the terrible events in Europe and Asia.

Although we listened to the news reports, read the papers and obeyed the blackout rules for shore homes, we were untouched by the horrors taking place abroad. We did not want to conjecture what we would do if Chick was drafted. We understood it could happen but this was today, what would be, would be.

We remained at the beach through September. When I returned to New York in early October I was in my ninth month and we were back to the lonely days and week-end visits. Happily Chick was with me for the delivery because I was smart enough to go into labor on the week-end he was home.

Our first son, Robert, was born November 2, 1942.

*Summer 1942*                    *Gloucester, Massachusettes*

*Rosalind*                          *Chick*

*September 1942, 8 months pregnant*

*Robert arrived November 2, 1942*

For two months after Robert was born, Chick continued to commute from Massachusetts to New York. The hated separation moved him to seriously consider finding another job so that we could be together and have a more structured life.

❖

## Sunday Afternoon

My Dearest Darling Wife,

I have just completed that call to New York and even tho it was brief it was so refreshing to hear your voice again and to hear that you and Robert are well again! It is snowing here and that makes everything seem all the worse. This life never did appeal to me and now I find that it is impossible!

The only solution is to get you here, or for me to quit my job and come to N.Y. But it's easier said than done. I do hope that I may be able to find a decent place here in town, whether Lowell or Boston or some suburb.

I have resigned myself to staying with the union for a while yet — until summer I guess — Those places I visited for jobs, — I made a swell impression in each — but always came a hairs breadth from actually getting the job. Bulova sent me a nice letter, and the fellow in Brooklyn told me that if I only had a little accounting experience he'd take me in a minute. Like this, he's going to wait a while to see if he can get someone that fills the bill exactly - He's in no particular hurry and can do that. If he doesn't find that guy — he'll take me — he says! The Bristol Co got in touch with me and said that they'd know in about ten days now. — He wanted to know if I was still available and that very frankly while he thought a great deal of me, there was one other fellow that he was also considering. — That in order to take me, they would have to overcome the hurdle that I have had no previous business experience.

So you see why I am not optimistic about the chances. They may yet come thru. I hope so.

Things are going along with the union but my approach has changed quite a bit. I am more easily irritated over small things that I never noticed before! Maybe that's merely a temporary condition. I was such a temperate fellow before — nothing around here ever bothered me.

I was happy to hear that Robert is well and happy. I don't seem to recognize him from week to week. How I envy you, your being with him day after day. Some day when he's old enough to understand, I shall tell him about his old man, and then about his wonderful mother — my only hope is that when he's old enough to see and hear, to walk and talk — that I'll be around to help him. To hold him and love him. How happy we'll all be when we get together.

There is not much more, except to say that I hope to see you really soon! Probably Friday late afternoon, if I can get away early enough. You have all my love dearest.

Always and Forever

> Kiss Robert for me oh so many times —
> Bye Darling
> CHICK

P.S. Have you gone to M.S.* clinic yet? Am sending only $5.00, more tomorrow — got to cash a check.

*M.S. - Margaret Sanger

Sun nite late

Dearest Rosalind,

I haven't been able to get the letter off yet not having either envelopes or stamps, but I'll send it special and put the Apt no. on it.

Soon, I'll be asleep and that will mark the end of a weekend, distinguished only for its loneliness and the abject sadness it brought. Lonely, without you — sad because of it.

I love you so much that I cannot face the prospect of being away from you and the baby. Sometimes, I feel that if someone pushed me I'd up and leave this place and take you and him away where we could start again — unknown — and try to make up for the past 2 ½ years. I could work at an ordinary job, an honest regular job and we could live a more peaceful orderly life. I'll never be rich anyway and tho I know we both like to have nice things and be very comfortable, still if they were hard to get, I know we could do without them —

But maybe it won't come to that!! At least we'll mark time for the present — we'll be together shortly after New Years — here or there — and try to snatch as much happiness as we can from life.

I look and see you and Robert all around me. You are always in my thoughts. At every turn I see you, smiling sweetly, so adorably and Robert is sleeping so peacefully and angelic. I shall have to go to sleep now and dream of you and me, and Robert living happily in a world of our own.

All my love Always
— CHICK —

The New York Times
Dec. 12, 1941, Dec. 9, 1941, Apr. 10, 1942, Nov. 8, 1942
*Courtesy of The New York Times Co.*

# The Army Years   1943-1946

The New York Times
July 1, 1943, Sept. 9, 1943
*Courtesy of The New York Times Co.*

# Chapter 6

## ON OUR OWN AND BACK AGAIN                    1943

B y February 1943, we were married two and one half years, and the housing shortage was still the thorn in our lives. Chick had moved up, from organizer in Fall River, to manager of the local ILG union in Lowell, Massachusetts. Desperate to find a place for us to be together, he scoured ads, saw real estate agents, questioned everyone he met, all without success. Apartments were as scarce as blue-eyed monkeys. Since 1941, all the country's resources had been relegated to the war effort. Iron, steel, aluminum, copper, lumber, every kind of building material as consigned and consumed in the building and production of guns, planes, ships, submarines, ammunition, army bases, air fields — anything related to defense.

The best Chick could find was a furnished room in a private home. The landlady worked the night shift at a factory producing war-related parts. She had an extra room and agreed to rent it out to this nice young man and his wife... A baby! — oh, that was a problem — because you see, she had to sleep all day. But if he would promise the baby wouldn't cry ...well then ... He promised.

My mother was not happy. This was not the dream world she wanted for me. How could I manage? There would be no kitchen, no place to move about; what kind of life was that? Even her cramped three-room apartment was better. "Your life," she said, "is supposed to be better than mine. Instead it's worse."

I did not agree. To me, it was a great adventure. Together, I was sure we could do anything. Besides we had to make this first move — we'd waited far too long already.

And so it was that we piled our car high with all our belongings, clothes for us, and the mountain of baby stuff for three-month-old Robert, and finally headed out together.

The six months that followed were hardly traditional. At the outset, when Chick called his office, he learned they wanted him to spend two weeks in Boston helping out in an organizing campaign. Without skipping a beat, we changed plans. Instead of destination Lowell, we headed for the Bradford Hotel in Boston.

We arrived at the modest hotel on schedule. The Bradford porter and desk clerk greeted us pleasantly. They actually appeared happy to see the baby; I felt welcome. A crib was set up in our room, which was not large, but quite comfortable. The bathroom was fair size and all ours. What a luxury!

Chick worked early mornings, lunch time and evenings, when he could see and talk with members while they were out of the factory. He could then spend several hours each day with Robert and me. We would drive to a staff member's home where I would make a 24-hour supply of baby formula. The hotel restaurant would refrigerate the bottles for us and all I had to do was call room service for a bottle as needed. The restaurant staff were great. Accommodating and friendly, they popped in from time to time to make sure I didn't need anything. I arranged for two weeks of diaper service and we were all set.

Robert was an astonishingly easy baby to care for. He always awakened smiling, ate on schedule and rarely cried. I could take him to the union office where he slept, gurgled and loved the attention of all the people who gathered around.

To add to our pleasure, some members of the cast of the musical comedy *Panama Hattie*, starring Ethel Merman, were housed on our floor. In a small friendly hotel like the Bradford, news travels and a three-month-old was rare. Soon a bevy of chorus girls came calling. "Do you really have a baby here? May we see him?" They came to ooh and ahh while offering me coffee and goodies from their rooms. Since Ms Merman was housed at a posh hotel, she missed all the fun. The two weeks flew by. It was my idea of heaven.

We moved on to our one room in Lowell, a far more confining space. No free run of the house or built-in visitors. The day we arrived I met the landlady. Short and stout. She reminded me how sensitive she was to noise and how much she needed her sleep all day. And yes, I could store the baby's bottles in the fridge. With that, she trundled off.

Since we couldn't use the kitchen facilities, Chick brought in some breakfast and lunch for me. We frequented a diner for supper and scoured the ads and bulletin boards for an apartment.

During the day all I could do was wheel the baby carriage around the working class neighborhood streets. Lined with single and two family clapboard houses, many seemed in need of repair. There were a few trees and bushes to soften the message of hard times. The February and March days were cold and windy and there were no parks or stores to investigate. People were keeping warm indoors. I made no friends. Still the strongest bonds were there. Chick and I were together. With the landlady working, the house was ours alone all night, and there was lots of time to enjoy this first baby.

After two months of searching, we found a one bedroom attic apartment high on Hungry Hill — a definite improvement. I settled into learning how to be on my own. But here again I was still isolated. The owners lived in the house, but they both worked. The hills were steep and negotiating the carriage up and down was exhausting. Mobility came only if you had a car — I needed a license. By July we had begun to make some friends and I had started driving lessons when Chick received the call from his draft board.

We were not unprepared. Men were being drafted in large numbers. More and more had already gone and all around us friends and acquaintances were now in service. Neither Chick nor I ever spoke of fear. Anxiety was the norm and conversation could only exacerbate those feelings. Instead, we each tried to get ready in our own way for what might be in store.

Chick spoke with his superiors to let them know what was happening and asked if he would have a job when he returned. He also queried friends about the induction process. I knew the apartment situation — not much choice there. I would move back with my parents and wait for developments. We would take it one day at a time.

The first step for Chick was to report to Camp Upton, New York. There he would go through his physical and be accepted, rejected, given a job at the camp, or assigned elsewhere. From now on we both had few choices. The U.S. Army would decide what to test, where Chick would go, and what he would do. I would follow wherever I could. No one could predict anything except that we were certain he would be accepted. Beyond that we thought of tomorrow or maybe next week. Never more than that. We expected he would get a week-end pass before he was shipped elsewhere.

When Chick was six, he crashed his left hand through a pane of window glass. Nerves, tendons, and blood vessels in his wrist were seriously injured. Surgery saved the hand, but his wrist remained underdeveloped and weakened all through his life — weakened enough so that the army medical staff, at Camp Upton, designated him non-tactical, unqualified for overseas duty and assigned him to the job of classification specialist. Since this meant a desk job, I was relieved. Chick was noncommittal. He hoped he would get his basic training in New York. After that I could join him, since it now looked like he would not be shipped overseas.

Robert was nine months old and we had been married three years when Chick was inducted on July 30, 1943. He was twenty-five years old when he began his active military service on August 20, 1943.

We learned only too quickly not to have expectations in the army. No week-end pass came through.

❖

Wed. nite

Dearest Ros and
Robert

This is rather a difficult letter to write. After several admonitions against thinking that I was sure to stay at Camp Upton for about 50 or 60 days, I still went ahead and

56

in my mind decided that I was to stay, and be in to see you several times before I was to leave N.Y.

Well, the Army has decided that this was not to be. When I got thru interviewing today — about 6:30, I learned that H.Q. was looking for me. When I reported there, I was told to go to the dispensary to get a medical exam, and that I was to be shipped out after breakfast. These are special orders affecting 18 men at the camp who are to be shipped to 4 or 5 different camps. The officers here don't seem to know much, or else they're not talking. So I have little idea where I'm heading. Of this tho, I'm rather certain. That the shipment will probably not be a Combat outfit. Those are always daily shipments of 300 men to one camp, and those shipments that consist of anything around 25 men or so who are notified in advance of shipment, are always "Specialists" sent to special jobs. I am wondering where I'm headed for. I hope its not too far! But everyone who has been here a long time, all tell me that it's a good shipment because only 5 or 6 men are going along with me.

I did so much want to get home to see you. So much that I only feel hatred and disgust toward the one who may be responsible for sending me out. Even tho it be a marvelous assignment, they shall carry my everlasting hatred with them, toward the grave.

I love you so much, and counted so much on being with you for a little while longer. Tho I did know that someday, I'd go —. Not to see Robert, whom I love so dearly, is a price too great to pay. Whoever keeps the books will have to be specially good to me before I consider them balanced. I shall no doubt be able to see you before too long. If I'm not too far away, you may be able to visit me. Don't worry too much about where I'll go or where I'll be. I shall be reasonably happy if the work is interesting. Think only that you have my love, Always and Forever.

Take Care of yourself and Robert. Lights are going out now.

>Leave you
>>with all my love
>>CHICK

❖

The scuttlebutt about Chick's placement was on target. He arrived at Jefferson Barracks (J.B.), Missouri, in September 1943, and within days other men assigned to the same unit straggled in. They came, one at a time, from different states around the country and seemed to have been individually selected for some special purpose. It was clear they had some obvious attributes in common. They were each between twenty-five and twenty-eight years of age, among the oldest group of draftees; all were college graduates credited with at least two degrees, some had earned their Ph.D. all were professionals. They wondered what plans were afoot for such an uncommon draftee group.

J.B. was an interim stop, a place for basic training. This usually meant six weeks of rigorous physical war preparation, a time for the men to learn to be soldiers. This group was old for the normal procedures, certainly not an outdoorsy crowd. They could see themselves bullied by the young eighteen-to-twenty-year-old sergeants and lieutenants, run ragged through the paces. Years away from their college days of sports, most of them never chose the sporting life. Out of shape and worried, as they waited, their active imaginations ran riot trying to guess what dreadful fate awaited them. They supported each other with outrageous stories of getting lost in bivouac, falling ignominiously while rope climbing, or some crazy idea they might be sent to classify K.P. details. The army was unpredictable; it was better to joke about it than try to figure it out.

When the last of the men arrived, they were quickly assembled for a briefing session. The truth was more surprising than anything they could have imagined. The U.S. government was looking ahead, examining some of the problems they would face at the end of the war. Eventually, millions of G.I.s would be eligible for discharge from the armed services. How to do it quickly and efficiently? All would need transportation; many would need medical care, time to readjust to civilian life and most important — JOBS. To avoid the chaos that could erupt from the repatriation of so many so quickly, the government was planning an employment and placement guidance service. Men ready for discharge would be reclassified, and the employment service would be ready to help them find civilian jobs. This group of well educated, well trained classification specialists were the core of the evolving plan.

They would have to take basic training, but would not be expected to do all the rigorous physical activity required of younger men. And since they would not face combat, they would receive only bare-bones instruction.

After the briefing, the consensus was, "It's too good to be true." It was.

The two letters here made me smile at his light-hearted style and left me with a fierce longing to see him.

❖

Tues nite

Dearest Ros - Robert

| | | |
|---|---|---|
| 5:15 to 5:35 | — | Rise and shine (shave optional), toilet seat, (10 min, on line) |
| 5:45 to 6:15 | — | Chow |
| 6:20 to 7:00 | — | Sweep hut and Mop. Hang up clothes, see that everything is ship-shape, Brush teeth and wash face, comb hair. |
| 7:00 to 7:30 | — | Stand formation while Sgt. Reads off list of details (work squads) and other announcements |
| 7:30 to 8:15 | — | Concentrated Calisthenics |
| 8:15 to 8:30 | — | Commando Course (that's murder) |
| 8:30 to 11:30 | — | Walk and run 2 miles — then 2 and one half hrs of drill |
| 11:30 to 12:30 | — | Chow and mail call |
| 12:30 to 3:00 | — | Drill |
| 3:00 to 4:00 | — | We cleaned a few streets, picked up papers |
| 4:00 to 4:30 | — | Wash and change uniforms |
| 4:30 to 5:00 | — | Mail call and announcements |
| 5:00 to 5:45 | — | Chow |

The day ends here — officially. However we still have to shine shoes, write letters — go to the Post Exchange to buy soda, soap, hangers, cigarettes, etc. Then we are to shave for next day and about 1 and one half or 2 hrs are really free to go to the Service Club or Day Room to sit around — yesterday was my first day of the above program. Today my second, and I'm going to sleep at 8:30 again tonite.

I hope that you can come out to St. Louis altho I'd think twice about bringing Robert. I still didn't get a chance to check on a Hotel with crib, but they say there are cribs in all of them. I shall speak to the Rabbi anyway and see if he can help me make arrangements!

If I know anything of definite value I shall call you again. I call at 7:00 and it's 8 in N.Y. We lost an hour somewhere on the trip out west.——I hope to hear from you by Friday as to whether you'll be out here. If things look promising from your reply and my investigations, I'll call you either sometime Sat nite or Sun during the A.M. so stay close to home Sun forenoon.

All my love sweetheart, to you and Robert.

—CHICK—

Wed. Aft—

Dearest Darling Rosalind

Feeling much better now! Last nite the gang was notified that we were to be on K.P. today. We all thought that we were thru with that for a while, but you know that you can't figure on anything in the army. I looked forward to a simply lousy time in the kitchen but I got a break because our Sergeant was "Charge of Quarters" last nite and knowing of my condition, he took my name off the list and ordered me to report to sick call. So I slept very well last nite, and saw the Doc in the AM —- No fever, slight cough, and nose clearing up. So he gave me pills and drops etc. — and off I went. Inasmuch as the gang is K.P. —therefore I play hide and seek with myself.

I am now in the midst of a wonderful "goof-off." After writing I shall try to take a nap - If nobody thinks of me, why then I'll be O.K. If they look for me, and find me, I'll tell them I took the medicine and dropped off to sleep!

There are many things I didn't write you about the Bivouac. Here are some interesting ones: When we reached our destination — (10 mi) we pitched tents. Our group (40) were near the River - the other group (40) were across a road — 100 yds away. After that we dug "straddle trenches" for use as latrines. They are 6 ft long — 4 ft deep and about 16 or 18 inches wide. Now they are used thusly. If one wants to urinate, then you stand near it and go to it. If you are thinking of otherwise relieving yourself you do as follows. After getting your pants and underwear down, you plant both feet, one on either side of the trench, then you sqat down slowly and gently making sure of your footing. Then when you are set, you let yourself to — Now you can't stay in that position very long — case your knees go. So you move fast, and button up — after using some tissue that you were foresighted enough to bring along.

After we got settled we ate, and it was swell chow. Then they called us together and said that we were going to get night problems — scouting and patrolling etc. Boy were we disgusted but our Lieut. was a swell kid. He called the other Lt. a boy scout for even suggesting it (not to his face —but to me and the Sgt.) and he went over to speak to him. As a result they decided to give us the nite off, and build a campfire.

Since the Lt. was so nice, we decided to give him a drink of Snake Bite Remedy (nee Scotch) that I and 2 others, (foresightedly again) were supplied with. It was a cold nite and the Lt. and the Sarge. and the two others and Me, sat in the tent, taking the necessary protective measures vs SNAKES!!

Then after some Horseplay — we went to sleep — and I might add that instead of Scouting and Patrolling at night and next AM there were several poker games and crap games — first time I saw that since I got in the army.

Right now it doesn't look at all as if we're going out on Bivouac again. But you know the army.

Well now — I haven't gotten anything from you today yet, but I may get a letter in PM mail call. Anyway you've been writing rather regularly. You're entitled to a little time off.

Nothing new at all about shipment. Hope to hell they get going soon. Its getting cold at J.B. altho it is warmer today - yet windier.

Hope you and Rob are well. You have all my love —
    Always Forever
      So much of it.
        CHICK

The New York Times
Dec. 25, 1943
*Courtesy of The New York Times Co.*

Chapter 7

# "MURPHY'S LAW" AT EVERY TURN      1943-44

After basic training, Chick spent several months at Jefferson Barracks waiting for his assignment. No one heard anything about the demobilization plan. The base knew nothing as Washington made the decisions. The boredom of waiting was nerve wracking. Chick could easily get an overnight pass to leave the base and pleaded for me to visit. I longed to go, but how could I manage it?

Back in the Bronx, my life was far from dull. Robert, now one year old, was walking — really running about. On the move, curious — see, an egg breaks when you drop it, look how this glass jumps when I bang it. He was into everything and testing everyone. He needed constant watching and we needed a structured day with many activities to keep him busy and out of trouble. He rarely napped mid-day and often stayed up past 8:30 or 9:00 PM. My parents adored their grandson and spent many hours reading and playing with him.

My mother and I had a non-aggression pact. She would take care of the house and food shopping, and I would chase after Robert and see that he caused the least damage to her knick-knacks and other belongings. A more than fair arrangement. Asking her to care for Robert all on her own was definitely not part of the bargain.

"You wanted a child, you have to take care of him," she would remind me. Alongside this attitude lingered a deep-seated fear of something terrible happening while she was in charge. She knew how quickly accident and illness could strike. My sister's death and Chick's brother's death were constant reminders. How could I ask her to do it?

The thought of taking Robert on a long train trip for a short visit to St. Louis was hair raising. The packing alone for a one-year-old was a turn off and managing him in a hotel room at this age was unthinkable. Chick and I would spend so much time chasing him, it would simply add to our frustration. I decided to discuss it openly with my mother.

I told her of Chick's pleading letter, and how important it was for me to see him. The look on her face told me she desperately wanted to say no to my request — but how could she? It was wartime and she was keenly aware that he might be assigned overseas duty. I watched her wrestle with her fears, her eyes full of pain. I left the room to give her some space and time to work it out with herself. When I returned she seemed calm. She looked up, sighed deeply and agreed to take care of Robert for up to two weeks.

Before I could leave for the trip, tragedy stuck at home. Chick's brother Eli, now 9 years old, became ill. Misdiagnosed as a case of the flu, he began to exhibit the terrifying symptoms we remembered too well: raging fever of over 105, excruciating headache, inability to move his head — the dreaded meningitis again. He was rushed to the hospital a day too late. Although penicillin had come on the scene, it was not readily available everywhere. Septicemia (blood poisoning) set in.

On October 8, 1943, the Army permitted Chick to fly home. He arrived in time to see Eli in the hospital, cradle him briefly, and watch him die in his arms. Weeping, I tried to comfort Chick as he sobbed uncontrollably for his brother's life and his parents' shattered dreams.

Following the funeral, Chick's leave was extended several days allowing us a short period of mourning and an opportunity to talk about ourselves. I told him I was afraid he couldn't live with the rigid army controls and military dogma that allowed no dissent or discussion. He said, "that's the easy part." As long as he could look forward to our life together, he could do it. "Whatever comes my way, I can take it."

In turn, he worried about my life in cramped quarters. "I can get out when Robert gets too rambunctious — escape to the park or playground — just let him run it off," I said. My mother often worried about Robert, but I could live with that. "It's not so hard," I told Chick. "It won't last forever."

We talked about the near future. If he remained non-tactical, then wherever he was sent, I could join him. Oh, how I wanted that! The army did not provide housing for non-commissioned married men,

*Eli Yale Chaikin 1934-1943*

but as long as he remained in the U.S., Robert and I could live off the base. Chick would then be allowed an overnight pass most evenings, depending on the rules of the unit. Just like a job, he would report back the next day, always in uniform. Everything depended on his assignment and physical assessment.

Before we were ready, it was time to say good-by again, a wrenching moment for me, harrowing for Beckie and Sam. They were devastated but stoic. Eli's death added heartbreak and depression to the dreadful moment. All we could do now was wait to hear if Chick would remain in the states.

On his return to Jefferson Barracks, Chick learned that the grand plan for demobilization had been premature. The war in Europe was far from won. The war in Asia, which engaged the Chinese, Indian and British armies along with the Americans, was both difficult and complex, and needed full attention. Many thousands of soldiers were being sent to fight the Japanese along with those still needed for the planned European invasion.

By this time we knew only too well that despite the careful interviews given at induction, military assignments had nothing to do with your background and experience. At any given time a new unit would be in formation and men were assigned willy-nilly to fill the jobs of that unit. A man trained in radar might find himself sent as a mail clerk. If a request went out for men who had a driver's license, (not everyone had one in those days), you knew not to volunteer.

Chances were good, went the joke, that you'd be given a wheelbarrow to push around all day.

Thus, when the full employment and placement guidance service was scrapped, these trained capable men knew they were "up for grabs" and could be assigned anything, anywhere. Chick was not surprised at the change, but we were both disappointed. It had been such an intelligent plan, and one that would be needed in time.

The unit was disbanded and each member given a new assignment. In November, Chick was assigned to the Sedalia Army Air Force Base just east of Warrensburg, Missouri. Then it was wait, wait, wait again. Fortuitously, he was granted permission to come home for a week, once more, before reporting to his new assignment.

We spent much of the leave with Beckie and Sam. Still grieving, the best balm for healing was Chick. In addition, we needed to help choose a head-stone for Eli's grave and set a tentative date for the unveiling. Though not a happy visit, every day we were together was such a gift. When he left, we knew we were in for more and more uncertainty.

January 30, 1944, Chick returned to the service and was actually transferred to Sedalia as a classification specialist. A few days later this letter came.

❖

Warrensburg, Mo
Feb. 12, 1944


Dearest Darling Ros:

Its rather quiet now — most of the boys are out of town, and this is the thing I've been waiting for. Just a chance to sit down and think of you and to let my thoughts float around a bit. Somehow in the last few months and especially when I was home recently, I never did get around to telling you, (in the way I imagined myself telling you), how much you mean to me and how very much I love you. Always when I write to you, in a quick fleeing second, I think of how I shall tell you. And when the words do hit the paper they don't seem the same. And when I was in New York, there always seemed something to do, something else to talk of, and then there was always Rob to keep us busy.

I have wanted so much to tell you quietly and sincerely that you are so much a part of me, that I can't visualize a life anywhere without you. That I love you so much, that every day without you is a day best spent in just existing. That I look back on the days that have gone by and heave a sigh of relief. That to look ahead is only to invite a feeling of despair, because I know it will be so long before I am with you again. And when I do happen to think ahead, and glow all over because I see myself beside you, it exhilarates me for a moment and then I bounce back to the reality. It is such a long, long way to the end of the rainbow.

Can I now tell you how much I wanted to walk with you, aimlessly in the evening and then sit on a bench somewhere and look around at the heavens, all aglow, and the ever smiling moon, and then at you who surely are brighter than heaven's brightest star, for the warmth of your glow warms my heart, even at such a great distance. And isn't it true that stars are not warming at all? Can I say now those things which my heart has been saying to you over and over again? Can I ever put down on paper the words to strange tunes I would be humming all thru the evening?

But tho I can not now repeat them, you can fill in the blank spaces. Think back to the times when we did walk and find a few seats overlooking the reservoir. Try to recall the things my heart thought of and my lips said. Try to imagine too, the kisses and caresses that would accompany all of this.

And if you can, then you will know of my love, and how great it is. My only hope is that I'll be able to somehow get settled at this base so that in a little while when the weather warms up, you will be able to come out with Rob.

I took the overseas physical with the others and I was told by someone who might know that I didn't make it on account of my hand. The procedure now is to appear before a Medical Reclassification Board. It's composed of 3 or 5 doctors. It's tough as hell to get by them. In my case, it's a tossup. But we shall see. If the board approves the findings of the doctor, then you are NON TACTICAL. That means you don't go over, and in all probability remain at Sedalia, and if they make you "TACTICAL" then the odds are that you're not at Sedalia long and that you'll go over eventually. Now again there's nothing to do but wait. Don't say anything to the folks about it all. The chances are that I'll be passed by the board and the entire thing would be just a tempest in a teapot.— I've got the feel of the work now and it's going along nicely. I can safely say that there's not much that I can find fault with at this Base. Of course when the memory of J.B. begins to dim, and I sort of get accustomed to this place, I'll probably begin to think that there's plenty wrong. The weather is warmer and I look forward to seeing it warm up some more.

Now that I've gotten some stamps, I'll try to get the letters coming to you on time.

You have all my love, kiss Rob millions for me. You have all my love!

Forever

CHICK

P.S. I can recall spending a few happier Feb 12th's than this one has been Remember?

❖

The days from January 1944 to April of that year became an endless drag. We were in limbo. I was aching to pack up and leave for Missouri, but without knowing Chick's status, the unpredictable army could reclassify him, pack him up and move him out just as I arrived. There could be no worse scenario. I stayed put.

Robert kept boredom at bay and moved the days along with new and unexpected surprises. He was fifteen months old and growing fast. New words spilled out daily. We were into learning body parts and I spent lots of time teaching the word "gentle." He would twist my nose as if to pull it off and say, "Noose" or poke my eyes, "ize," to show where they were. Each time I would have to say, "be gentle, that hurts, gently, gently..." and show him how he should do it. His hearty laughter was infectious and soon we'd be rolling on the floor playing "looking for your laughing place." I knew just where to tickle and it would catch him by surprise sending him into fits of laughter. My mother would come to break it up. "I don't know which one is the baby here."

In the park, he'd notice the trees and the changing leaves. He had learned to walk at eleven months and by this time, running was his favorite sport. That was fine in the park, but keeping him in check on the city streets became my daily exercise.

Once or twice a week, we went to visit Sam and Beckie. Since Eli's death, they lived lives of quiet desperation, and though Chick wrote to them, they always asked, "Where is Chick? What does he write? Is he well?" Sam never believed Chick would survive the service; Beckie had greater faith in life's goodness. Robert brought laughter and fun into their house but his perpetual motion left them weary.

Chick could call me occasionally, but I could not call him. Phone conversations were so unsatisfactory. What could we say? Our cheerful words rang false, and overwhelming longing washed over us afterwards. Letters were so much better. We read and reread the words and writing them filled the long uneventful evenings — they were our visiting time.

Finally all the army tests were done and Chick called with the news I wanted to hear.

Chick's official medical military records of February 14, 1944 states: "Unqualified for overseas duty; injury to nerves, tendons and blood supply of ulna side of left wrist; recommend retention of Non-Tactical assignment."

This issue settled, I was ready to pack my bags and move, but that was not to be. The Sedalia Army base was being consolidated into one enormous air-force outfit and would become a training replacement base for the Troop carrier Command. Rumors were rampant. "They" said that every enlisted man on the base would be sent overseas. "They" were going to Europe for the 2nd front; no, "they" were going to India for the Pacific war; no matter where, "they" were definitely going.

Chick knew that a large combat cargo command group was being assembled to be shipped out soon. The base was all a flurry and he cautioned me to wait for things to settle down. By the end of March, I was beginning to fear that we were losing whatever days we could have together. With my patience and longings stretched ragged and with Chick pleading once again for me to visit, albeit alone, I spoke with my mother again about looking after Robert. Without hesitation this time, she said, "You have a rain check. Use it."

I was off to Warrensburg, Missouri at last; not as I had pictured it, with Robert to stay, but grateful as all get-out for this two week reunion. Chick met me at the station with a GI friend who owned a car. What a luxury! We were dropped at a small, genteel, European style hotel in town. The charming flowery logo told me everything I needed to know. European Plan —HOTEL ESTES, C.R. SHRIVER OPERATOR, $1.00 to $2.00. Chick had done some homework and the desk clerk was alerted. Smiling warmly, he greeted us with open southern charm and a border-state accent, not deeply southern, but pleasantly twangy. Despite the crowds of GIs and their visitors hovering about, the personnel always kept their voices soft and spirits cool.

Chick had a three-day pass. We dined quietly in the hotel restaurant that first night, caught up on all the news. I had brought pictures and messages from home, Chick had letters from cousins stationed elsewhere. We clung to each other like newlyweds and reveled in the complete privacy and love we had missed for seven months. I told him how I hated being apart, how I missed him, how we just had to take advantage of whatever time we had to be together. Chick said he had a furlough coming in May, and it looked unlikely that he would be affected by any of the changes taking place at the base. He would find an apartment for us, come east on furlough, and we would all three return together.

C. R. SHRIVER, OPERATOR
$1.00 TO $2.00

As the days flew past, I was torn between wanting to stay and my growing anxiety each time I thought of my mother at home with Robert. Parting, as always, was heart wrenching. But this time there was so much hope we would be together again soon. It was looking good.

As soon as I walked into the Bronx apartment I was distracted from the emptiness I felt on leaving Chick. My mother had survived very well. My father, always supportive, had outdone himself. He normally worked until nine at night but during this time he reorganized the factory schedules and for the first time ever, he arrived home early enough to be with Robert and help my mother through dinner. He actually took Saturday as well as Sunday off. His added attention meant they could get to the zoo as well as the park and playground and visit with Chick's parents too.

Not a bad outcome, I thought, and felt my guilt slip away at their tales of good times together.

Robert's reaction however, caught me unaware. When I walked in, his eyes lit up. A smile started to form when, in a flash, he switched off his pleasure, turned his back and refused to look at me. He would not allow me near him. I had abandoned him and he was not about to forgive me easily. There were no hugs or kisses. He would slap his hands against his ears not to listen. But when I said I would take him out to the park, it was an offer he couldn't resist. It was the first step to forgiveness, but he had learned to be wary.

A week after I returned, Chick wrote that the base policy regarding furloughs had changed, leaving us high and dry with our plans for May. Dismayed, I decided not to wait any longer, and made plans to leave by May 10th. Chick's folks decided to accompany me. They would visit for a week, but I would stay on.

It seemed as though Murphy's Law was kicking in at every turn. Whatever could go wrong did — Robert came down with chicken pox. The doctor insisted I would have to wait for all the pox scabs to disappear. Sam and Beckie decided not to postpone their trip and took off without me. I was horn-mad. I raged with self pity. "Why am I so unlucky?" I moaned. My father would have none of that. "Never say such a thing," he said. "You're very lucky. You'll see, I'm right." I found his words strangely comforting.

The chicken pox came and went; I packed my bags in a trice, bundled Robert up (now 1 year 7 months) and moved to Warrensburg, Missouri. The train trip from New York was standard war-time confusion. It would take more than 30 hours to arrive in Warrensburg.

More and more soldiers were now in transit, and there were no assigned seats on the train. Every seat was taken when I boarded in New York. Soldiers and civilians crowded into the aisles, sat on suitcases, arms of seats, squeezing three where two should be. The air hung heavy with anxiety. You could see it in the faces of the soldiers, and the fretful eyes of women and men all through the long and arduous overnight ride. Yet, with all the discomfort, I remember only the smiles and care of all aboard. We were in this together, and everyone took turns sitting, standing, leaning, crouching. No tempers flared, no prima donnas surfaced. As a young mother, I was treated with extra care. So many volunteers, always ready to let the toddler sit, lie down, climb about.

Robert was lively and verbal, friendly to a fault. He wandered the car making friends, laughing, enjoying the people and the attention. In turn, he provided a cheerful diversion for the adults. They told him stories, played games, and when sleep caught him of a sudden in my lap, they offered to hold him from time to time so I might rest a bit. Although I can recall only a bit of the hardship of that interminable ride, I remember vividly the kindness that each passenger shared with me and each other. Just knowing Robert and I would be together with Chick, for whatever time the fates would permit, was enough to keep the tiredness from taking over as we traveled.

From my trip in April, I knew that Warrensburg would be a wonderful town for us. Chick had lucked into a bright, spacious one-bedroom furnished apartment in a private house. The other rooms had been converted into one-room studios and were also rented to army wives. Chick could leave the base each evening about five P.M. and return early the next morning. He had Sundays off, K.P. once a month, and one three-day pass a month. Finally, ten months after his induction into the army, we could settle into a family life.

I can still feel the warmth of that large, airy kitchen. It became the focus of activity for the few friends we met, who came with their wives and children to sit around our table and eat, drink and talk war and army life.

I learned very quickly that Warrensburg was famous for three things: its proximity to Independence, Missouri, its dirt cellar floors, and its huge, voracious roaches. Once I found a way to draw a line the roaches would respect at the entrance to my apartment, life was easy. All it took was spreading a liberal amount of boric acid inside the kitchen cabinets and across the entrance door — a trick my mother used in New York City apartments.

Missouri State Teacher's College, within walking distance of our apartment, had a nursery school and playground. Robert was too young for school but we were able to use the play equipment at will. He loved the swings and slide and the easy access to the open campus. A perfect change from the streets of New York City.

During the four months in Warrensburg, we were glued to the radio reports of the war on all fronts and read every newspaper. The Asian war was raging as the European war seemed to be nearing a climax, (actually, it had more than a year to go). In the China Burma India (CBI) Theater, the brutal fighting demanded more fighting men, more specialists, more pilots, more supplies. By July, Chick saw the tempo at the base speeding up and began to feel that his number would inevitably come up for overseas assignment. He was sweating out his October furlough, hoping against hope he would get the fourteen-day-leave.

In late September Chick announced that we should get ready for his furlough and take a trip back home. I was taken aback when he suggested we pack most of our stuff, and suspected something was going on. "No," he said. "I've got one coming, if we don't take it, we could lose it."

I was suspicious about this sudden move since Chick always said that changes took place on the base "the minute your back was turned." But we did want to see our folks. Besides, the unveiling of

Eli's gravestone was also due to take place. We wanted to be there for that.

What I did not know was that the 4th Combat Cargo Group was being assembled out of the Sedalia Air Base for shipment overseas. They would need a classification specialist. His non-tactical status prevented the assignment, but though his hand had not changed, it was not a significant handicap for the job he would need to do. Taking the furlough was a keen idea while the army decided how to handle the problem. They would not approve the leave once the decision was made.

On our way to New York City he told me he might be recalled. I was not surprised. We spoke for a long time about an overseas assignment. As always, his confidence in himself reassured me. He expressed no fear. There was a part of him that wanted to be more actively involved in the fight, just as another large piece longed to stay home with us.

I resolved not to worry about what might happen. After all, he could get assigned to another base in the U.S. Still an optimist, I believed there was a chance this change could lead to something good. Once again there was nothing to do but wait. There was one thing I never questioned — if he left, he would survive and return. I never considered any other possibility.

On October 17, 1944 to fill the needed complement of the group, the army changed Chick's status from Non-Tactical to Qualified For Full Field and Overseas Duty. He was promptly assigned to the 4th Combat Cargo group, the 15th Squadron for overseas duty.

The New York Times
June 5, 1944, June 27, 1944
*Courtesy of The New York Times Co.*

The New York Times
June 4, 1944, Aug. 26, 1944,
*Courtesy of The New York Times Co.*

The New York Times
Oct. 1944
*Courtesy of The New York Times Co.*

Chapter 8

## READY FOR THE DAYS AHEAD 1944

I was stunned when we received the call in the Bronx for Chick to report back immediately. Though Chick had tried to prepare me, I had clung unrealistically to the hope that his non-tactical status would keep him stateside. The phone call left me shaken. It was too soon. I was not ready. Ridiculous thoughts flashed through my mind. Maybe I could pack up and follow? I wiped the fantasy away and quickly settled into reality. I felt weak and unsteady. Chick held me close, "Ros, don't worry, we'll get through this."

Chick returned to his base, and was ordered to leave at once for Bowman Field, in Louisville, Kentucky. The first chance he had he sent this letter.

❖

Tuesday Nite
Bowman Field

Dearest Darling Ros,

Today went by quickly again with my clothing check (They gave me many brand new clothes) and the Colonel's inspection in the P.M. So at six o'clock with no appetite for anything at all, I went to the show on the base, and it was terrific. I haven't seen such lousy pictures in God knows when.

I still haven't gotten any mail! I do so hope I hear from you tomorrow A.M. Today the C.O. announced that he would let 10% of the men go on a 3-day pass starting Wed.nite to be back Sun. A.M. But he stipulated that they be given to the men who haven't been home since June, and further he set a 500 mile limit. He is such a bastard that I'm sure he won't let me go on pass. Anyway it takes 22 hrs to get down to New York, and at that rate, I wouldn't even have a day with you. Right now we're pretty certain of staying here till Monday or so. How many days past Monday I cannot say. Not many I'm sure. I hope you have given serious thought to coming down here and have arrived at a definite answer. If you can come down, then you will have to do so almost immediately. If you feel that you can't leave Robert and can't come with him, that's all right, sweetheart, for I know how much you want to come, and that only Robert could keep you from me and he is also worth all the love and attention you can give him. I shall call you anyway Thurs. nite, for I expect you to get this Thurs. AM, and you can answer me then.

Since I have had no news from the outside world, this note will be shorter than usual. The Airdrome Squadrons that are attached, one to each Combat Cargo Sq. are leaving Bowman for Baer Fld; the P.O.E. for these outfits — one at a time, (one a day) starting Thurs. By Sunday they will be gone. Generally, the airdrome squadrons leave 30 days or so before the Cargo Sq. because they travel by water and they are supposed to have everything set for us when we get over. But there are rumors that they will be flown over too, therefore my pessimistic attitude toward the length of time we'll be here. All the training is practically over and all that's left is to sit around and wait to take off. That's tough to do.

While I'm writing this, Bob Hope is on the radio and I can only half follow him. I will be hearing him often these next months, and it will be strange, for I know that you'll be listening too, and we'll be worlds apart; in distance at any rate. For the rest, I'll be close to you ever, for I carry you in my heart.

Soon now I'll go to town to do a little shopping for Rob's birthday. I look forward to getting him something he'll get some fun out of.

So here we are again, starting a grand new adventure. Grand only in terms of size. For the rest of it, I say its spinach and to hell with it. I hate the thought of leaving, of living alone, and of being in the army. But I shall try to keep interested in reading and writing and I look forward to that seeing me thru. I love you so much, O, So very, very much. — Millions and millions of hugs and kisses for both of you

Love me Forever, as I do you — CHICK

❖

As soon as I learned I could see him I decided to go there. Once again the question was whether or not to take Robert. This time I decided I could not leave him home. He would be two years old in another week and he might not see his Dad again for a year, maybe more.

When I told Chick's folks I was going to Kentucky, Sam made plans to join me. I knew he would. Though he did not speak of it to me, he had told others that he was convinced this was the last time he would ever see Chick again. He had lost two sons and now his eldest would be taken also. I tried to cheer him up on route, assuring him that Chick would return. It was easy to say — I believed it absolutely.

We had two days in Kentucky. Keeping our emotions under control was the only way we knew to get through the days. Sam accompanied us everywhere; his face grim, always on the verge of tears, his eyes glued to Chick as though he hoped to trace every feature.

Fortunately, Robert kept us amused, reminding us, as only a child can, that there was a future. Even Sam laughed when Robert wore Chick's hat everywhere, even though it came down to his nose, or when he played hide and seek at every turn. When he asked Chick "Where you goin' Daddy?" we said we didn't know and laughed as we tried to teach him the slogan of the day, *Loose Lips Sinks Ships*, a tongue twister he could not master.

I cannot remember where we ate or at what hotel we stayed. Throughout the days I kept telling myself that every passing minute was a moment gone. The days were flying by, even though each hour seemed like an eternity. Conversations were nonsense — just words to fill the time and we were wasting it. Chick would not talk about where he believed he was headed and I would not ask. Chit-chat about this one and that one made my eyes glaze over, but when our eyes met, I could not keep my gaze steady without falling apart. There was a piece of me wishing this ordeal was over, that I was on my way home. Saying good-by was going to be unbearable. This time we knew the war had to end before we could be together again.

Happily, Robert slept soundly that night. Though ours was a sleepless night, Chick and I were finally alone together. There was enough time to savor the last precious moments, listen to the voice of love, and reject gloom.

For fourteen months, from the day Chick left Bowman Field to when he boarded ship for his return trip home, we wrote each other every single day. The letters were threads that fashioned an unbreakable bond, keeping despair in check as they wove a fabric of renewed hope for our future — again and again and again.

Chick often complained about the army mail delivery system. To make sure we received every letter each of us sent, we took to numbering them. The system proved that the army was totally reliable — not one went astray.

After I had received almost one hundred letters, I realized I could not keep them all (after fourteen months I would have had over six hundred). With limited closet and drawer space in the apartment, it wasn't long before every available corner was stuffed. I decided to be selective. After reading and re-reading them many times, I found myself keeping every poem, and those letters where the language tugged at my heart, or searched his inner self, made me laugh, or drew word pictures of places he saw and people he met. Ever mindful of the censors and need for secrecy, his letters were circumspect, but the poems said everything.

Chick, on the other hand, had saved every letter of mine. At the end of the war, after fourteen months overseas, he returned home with duffel bags stuffed with hundreds of letters. The sight of them made me shudder. I considered my writing much inferior to his, particularly since there was so little of interest for me to report. I did not meet new and interesting people or travel to exotic places. The everyday events seemed mundane. I dreaded the thought of re-reading the daily skirmishes with Robert, my mother, or in-laws, and I certainly did not want to relive the longings and loneliness of those days. In a most thoughtless moment, I gathered them together and dumped them all into the apartment house incinerator.

Chick returned from an appointment that day and asked where I had put them. When I told him, the color drained from his face. He became chalk white, speechless. He turned away, sat down to read and never mentioned them again.

I was aghast. How could I have been so insensitive? Surely I should have known, no matter how badly written, they were his treasures, just as his letters were mine. Apologies were meaningless. My letters were gone, irretrievable.

*Ros, Chick and Robert, 1944*

Chapter 9

# 100 PLANES TAKE OFF — 97 ARRIVE          1944

In November 1944, I returned home from Kentucky and awaited the first letters. I did not know when the group would leave the country, and until they did, there would be no letters. It was important to keep that information top secret so that the enemy could not have easy access to the number of forces being deployed, or their comings and goings.

I have recently found a wonderful book entitled, *It Began at Imphal, the Combat Cargo Story* by John G. Martin D.V.M. (Published by Sunflower University Press 1988.)

It tells the story of the Combat Cargo concept and operations, and specifically describes Chick's group. As a result, together with *Combat Squadrons of the Air Force, World War II*, edited by Maurer Maurer, I have been able to put together the following overview of Chick's flight overseas.

One hundred planes and their crews took off for Asia on November 12, 1943. For security reasons they flew a circuitous route overseas. Their first stop was Borinquin Field, Puerto Rico where a C-46 damaged a wing and was left behind. The next stop at Georgetown, British Guyana, they spent the first of many hot nights sleeping under mosquito netting. The flight continued, as Chick tells us, to Belem and Natal in Brazil. From Natal they turned eastward, and after a long flight over water they reached the Ascension Island, a tiny outcrop of rock in the southern Atlantic Ocean. Then on to Accra on the gold coast of Africa, across the Sahara to Kano, Nigeria where a C-46 from the 13th squadron crashed, resulting in another aircraft loss but no injuries. The convoy continued to Khartoum in the Egyptian Sudan, then on to Aden where one of the 4th's planes crashed on take off killing five crew members and injuring nine passengers. The group continued along the coast of southern Arabia to Masira Island. The last leg of the journey brought them to Karachi, India where they rested for 2 days. Departing Karachi, most of the planes towed gliders across the Indian Desert, stopping for a short time at Agra, the home of the Taj Mahal. Some gliders were released at Ondal, the rest were towed on to Sylhet.

Of the original 100 planes, 97 arrived ready for service on December 1, 1944 in Sylhet, India, the new home of the 4th Combat Cargo Group. The overseas flight had taken 10 days to India, and several more to Sylhet.

Once the group was on its way overseas, there were several stops where the men could mail letters. It was such a relief when I received the first letters so much sooner than I had expected.

Here are some of Chick's comments and thoughts on the flight. He never mentioned the casualties on route.

❖

21 Nov. 1944 Brazil

Darling:

It was quite a nice trip down altho I've seen many new places and things from the air, the two events which stand out are these:

1. We crossed the Equator

2. I got a good long look at the Amazon River.

About five minutes before we crossed the Equator, the navigator came out to tell about it. And at the moment he figured we were over, on, or under it (I always did have trouble with imaginary lines) the radio operator proceeded to douse water over everyone's head. If it's crossed via steamship, legend has it, that all who cross for the first time rate a ducking. Our ceremony seems to have been adapted for and to air travel.

It hardly seems possible that we left the states just a very short time ago. But fast as it is, when I'm homeward bound, sometime in the fairly distant future, this will seem very slow.

I hope you get these letters regularly. If you do, why then it will be so much easier to wait for my cable when we get to our ultimate destination. And if you write regularly, why then I'll probably be getting a stack of letters from you.

The only bad feature of the trip thus far is the loss of my fountain pen. This morning before we took off — with hundreds of GI's milling around the barracks, I made the mistake of leaving it on the bed with my writing kit and hand-bag. Then when I cleaned up, we all made a rush for the flight line. On the way I discovered the pen's absence. I rushed back and looked around. It was gone. And this note is written with a borrowed pen.

Now if you have no great need for the other pen, and if you can put a new point on it, and if you think you ought to, why send it to me. Again, be thoroughly sure that it is packed well in cotton, if need be, for packages sent abroad usually get a good kicking around.

My appetite seems to have improved since we started the trip and despite the obvious heat, I have so far been very comfortable. One wonderful thing about this is that thus far it has been cool at nite. So much so, that up to now we've slept under blanket (1) and sheet. And another strange thing is the almost universal use of mosquito netting for the bed and atabrine pills. In a few weeks I expect to be saffron-colored. That is unless we're in one place long enough to get tanned by the sun.

It's difficult to stop thinking of you and Robert even for a few moments, the reason I guess is that I do nothing at all the entire day but ride in the plane and lay around in the barracks. They don't let us out of the bases, and so the one thing that would make this trip really interesting is lacking. But I manage to get some local color thru talks with GI's who have been stationed at these places for months and even years.

Will write you again tomorrow. You have so much of my love. I think of you for hours before I drop off to sleep. I love you so dearly. Millions of kisses for you and Robert-

Forever<br>CHICK

❖

The loss of the fountain pen was major. A good fountain pen was a precious possession, considered a wonderful gift for a Bar Mitzvah or Jr. High School graduation. Once chosen from the vast array of color, designs and sizes, you expected to keep it forever. In 1944, there were no ball points, no felt tips, no easy inexpensive way to replace the pen. With an income of $20 a month for Chick and $60 for me, the replacement was a cost item to think about.

❖

Sunday 26 Nov. 44

Darling:

We are in the middle of Africa, Nigeria, after a rather pleasant flight. Of all the ways of getting to our destination, the powers that be chose the one route thru Africa where there is little to be seen. Near all the army bases here are found native villages. Altho we were not allowed off the base, I picked up some local color in ordinary conversation with some of the men stationed at these African bases.

In West Africa, they tell me, few natives wear anything resembling clothes. Both males and females are nude, live in huts made of mud, sticks with thatched roofs. Pigs, goats and what not are in them, and no sanitary facilities whatever. One important reason for these towns being "off limits" is the superabundance of venereal disease and yet, if these stories are true, many of the boys around, take advantage of the presence of these native women. A soldier must care little for himself and less for his future, if he does.

At this base I was amazed to find, in the middle of the Dark Continent, a mess hall, reminiscent of a fine cafe in New York or Boston. And the food served, compared favorably with the fine food at the Toll House at Whitman, Mass. For dessert, they had "Banana Splits." Can you tie that! Real delicious ice cream with whipped cream and chopped nuts, plus the ever present banana. As a matter of fact, since we left Florida all we seem to get for fruit is "Banana and Orange"

About the barracks. They are large and comfortable and with the exception of one place since Florida, it has been cool every nite, and so "good sleeping weather." All the

91

cleaning up and making of beds is done by natives and to top it off, there's a large Frigidaire in each barracks where the men keep their bottles of beer. Last nite I went to the show and saw Atlantic City. It was outdoors and exceedingly pleasant. Again with but one exception all the theatres thus far are outdoor affairs, and the pictures start when the sun sets.

So much for Nigeria. We continue onward and as we do my thoughts turn evermore to you and my deep love for you. I hope you are writing fully about Robert. I miss you both so. Keep well and happy and write as often as you can. You have all my love,

Forever,
CHICK

Monday
27 Nov 44

Darling,

Tonight finds me somewhere in Egypt feeling really good. I have just showered and shaved and after this short note I shall head for bed.

Again I'm surely disappointed at not getting out to see the neighboring town, but I'm accustomed to that. Maybe one of these days I'll be able to really go sightseeing. We are bedded down tonite in what used to be an extraordinarily nice school, for Egyptians I guess. And tonite, literally, I'm sleeping under the stars, for about 50 of us are on the roof. It's cool, and since they supplied blankets why then, I look forward to fine sleeping weather again tonite.

There is something nearby to see, a fair to middling Egyptian town with, I'm told, 2 cabarets. But again no dice — no get out.

The trip is beginning to tire me. Hope it ends soon. For that matter I wish with all my might the whole damn war ends soon so I can come back to life again, with you and little Robert. I love you both so dearly. Look forward soon to reading letters from you. As I gaze upon the stars tonite there's none can compare with you.

All my love forever
CHICK

Wednesday 29 Nov 44

Darling,

We had a short and rather pleasant flight today and we find ourselves bedded down on an Island (somewhere off the coast of Arabia) and tomorrow we'll be at our ultimate destination.

This place is really primitive. If I didn't know the tremendous problem they have of getting supplies here, I'd say that the food is revolting. The latrines of pre-Biblical vintage etc. But since this is **war** (pronounced Wah) I'll just say that the chow is GI, and the quarters etc., leave only a little to be desired. But with it all, if the base where I might ultimately be stationed is no worse than this, I'll be happy. Whatever else, this place is bearable even tho the absence of mosquitoes is more than overshadowed by the abundance of large well fed flies.

Believe me, when I tell you that I've seen my belly full of this world. Nothing could please me more than to start home **now**!!

But you and I know that we have to "sweat" this war out. We shall both have to do the best we can.

I am exceedingly anxious to have this trip done with, and to feast my eyes on some mail from you. I keep looking at the moon and see your shining face. I love you so very much. All my love, Always and Forever. Millions of kisses for you and Robert.

Love,
CHICK

# Chapter 10

## NO SURPRISE — IT'S INDIA 1944

Chick did not write about the horrors of war, the cruelty or sickness he may have encountered. I saw no newspaper reports about the war in India. It was only later, through research, that I learned of these hardships.

On December 1, 1944, the 4th Combat Cargo Group arrived at Salutiker Air Field in Sylhet, India. The airstrip was surrounded by jungle, which swarmed with thousands of green parrots and trees full of screaming monkeys. At night the howling jackals prevailed, and the jungle floor crawled with mites, ticks, leeches, mosquitoes, new varieties of insects, not to mention cobras and tigers, subjecting the men to typhus, malaria, and Dengue fever. The climate was as much an enemy as the Japanese, making it a medical war as well. In early January, the monsoon rains pounded away creating additional havoc.

Inside their bashas the men contended with rats, and all kinds of crawling vermin. The natives they employed cleaned and helped keep things under control.

The 4th became one of the main carriers for the British troops. It was a first in aeronautic planning. Their purpose was to supply an army completely dependent on air support for its very existence. They carried provisions, equipment, ammunition, reinforcements and evacuated casualties. Over the year, as the British and Indian armies moved to take back the Burma Road, Mandalay, and Rangoon, the C-46s hauled war materiel and troops, rubber boats, a Bailey bridge, bombs, food, ammunition, gasoline, pontoons, and every tool and contrivance needed to fight the war.

This is how Chick describes his arrival and the town.

❖

Saturday
2 Dec 1944

Darling,

The flight is over and here we are. No surprise at all to me that we landed in India finally, in Assam Province, to be exact. On the whole, the trip was not too bad, but if I had any choice, I'd prefer any other mode of travel. Several days, during the trip, one of the engines threatened to cut out. And tho these planes can fly on one engine for as long as the gas holds out, yet the uncertainty of the remaining engine's ability to keep going gives rise to great alarm to all concerned. For when you're in the middle of the Atlantic, or the South American jungle, or the African desert, or the India waste land, you are really alone and the thought generally strikes home with great impact. All of these fears struck me several times during the trip when this engine sputtered and coughed and started to cut out. But we made it and that's that but I wouldn't care to take another try at it. You know that normally, except for that instinct at self preservation, I wouldn't care about taking chances via a parachute jump and a long trek to safety. But there is so much more to be reckoned. You and Robert are what I cherish and live for. If I thought for one moment that I wouldn't come back to you, life would be meaningless now. But since we look forward to a wonderful life together when this is over, in order to make sure of that expectation, I don't care to stick my neck out. I shall do what must be done, little else.

Now we are located here, for as long as the powers that be decide. And in that matter of my expectation, I am pleasantly surprised to find the food and quarters better than imagined. We live in shacks, native name "Basha", not sturdy, but constructed entirely of bamboo, with a brick floor and bamboo thatched roof. There are four of us in this one and we have a swell group of fellows. The beds are made of bamboo too, and I shall try to draw some pictures for you. I only hope that they convey the idea to you.

1. Looking down on bed.
And you'd be surprised
how springy the bed is.
The wavy lines are fine strips of bamboo interlaced.

2. The "Basha"
There's an overhanging roof
running along the front.
Provides shade! Good place to sit and talk of "home."

Shortly after we arrived, as seems to be the custom, we engaged the services of a native Hindustani. There are 4 men here. Total pay 28 rupees a month. In American money about $8.40. Think of it. He cleans our place up, makes and airs our bed, runs errands, makes things for us, cleans up our area and does everything that occurs to us to tell him to do. We get along somehow, for he seems to sense what we want done. And anyway he was well broken in by the men who came before us. Our little place, after only one day, really looks good. And we have further improvements in mind. This afternoon, we hied ourselves down to the village —— quite a town, almost beyond description, (but I shall tell you of it in later letters) and bought mattresses and pillows They are cotton filled, (pillows made of feathers) and very, very comfortable. Cost of 1 each — total 11 rupees, about $3.30 for both. I also bought a good leather wallet for 2 rupees (60c) and a mirror (30c or 1 rupee) and in spite of the fantastically cheap prices, we still overpaid about 40%. But with our initial experience with the native vendors has come a great deal of sagacity. A few more trips and we shall become expert hagglers. The prices are cheap enough, but they expect us to chew 'em down a bit. If we don't, they'll think ill of us and consider us 'pushovers." Some of the English soldiers stationed nearby explained that to us. You know me —"when in Rome, etc."

And for food, everything comes to us from a great distance, most of it "flown in." So while in the states, we might be impelled to throw the chow back at the mess sergeant, here, for an overseas outpost, it is considered to be pretty good. We do get fresh eggs, tho milk is exceedingly scarce, And often enough, the tinned meats, like Spam and roast beef hash make an appearance. But once our own mess is functioning the food will be better. All in all much better than I expected and generally much better than is found in this part of India.

This has been our first day here, since we arrived last nite. It was pleasant, exceedingly interesting. We know that there will be trying days ahead but for a while at least we are happy and by and large contented.

Only the thoughts of you and Robert and home dampen the spirits. I love you with all my being and hope so fervently that this will be over sooner than we dare think.

You are all my life and will be forever. Please take care of yourself. Stay well and happy. We are all looking forward to our first "mail call." None more eagerly than I. You have all my love -

—CHICK—

7 Dec 1944
Assam Province India

Darling,

Another day and still no mail!! Only the certain knowledge that somewhere, between this outpost and home, there's some mail from you keeps me going. I keep telling myself that you and Rob are well and that helps. As for me, I'm fine.

Today, I awoke with a tough headache and it stayed with me all day. Right about noon I tried to take a nap but couldn't drop off to sleep. In recent months they have come more frequently than ever before. But I suppose this one is due to the fact that since arriving here I've been reading a lot and writing a good deal by candlelight. As a result, I guess my eyes suffered some strain. But since they have set up the portable generator, and wired the area, we ought to have some light tomorrow. That ought to do the trick for I know that I won't read or write less, unless we run out of reading material. And apropos, should you send a package, and should you have any *Time, Newsweek,* or *Saturday Evening Posts* lying around, you might do well to throw those in.

There wasn't much doing today and I was grateful for that, what with the headache, but I did contrive to get a long letter off to Sol. I hope I can get one off to Larry tomorrow. Haven't been to town except for that first time but the memory is still pretty vivid. I shall make an effort to describe the main thoroughfare.

There is a road, somewhat like those found in the Catskill Mt area, wide enough for two cars and tarred, which runs thru the camp and after 5 miles becomes the main drag. The outskirts of town are delineated by markers reading "Built up area, speed 20 mi per hr." Once that sign is passed, it is all a driver can do to avoid slaughtering hundreds, even at a rate of 5 mi per hr. For one thing there are no sidewalks and the natives, thick as the proverbial fleas merely stroll on the road totally unconcerned. One needs to keep the horn honking continuously.

Most of the native transportation consists of a taxi-like affair, sort of a 2 seater hansom carriage, powered by a bicycle. The driver merely pedals merrily along carrying his fare behind him. For the rest, ox-cart is extensively used. And here and there a cow and some goats wander around on the roads. There are blocks of shops of every kind, with one thing in common! They stink!! Whatever food there is offered for sale is dirty, rotten-smelling and certainly indigestible. It's worth your life to eat or drink anything sold in town.

Many other shops sell a variety of things useful to G.I.'s. I have already made mention of the mattress shop. This place was about 6 feet wide and 60 ft deep. In the front of the shop are 3 or 4 natives seated on the floor (earth), beside a pile of completed mattresses. Further back, a native workman is stitching the sides of a mattress with a long needle. He sits cross-legged and works very quickly. The stitching is such as to create a quilt effect in the mattress. Farther back are several men seated before a mound of cotton, (raw) and they seem to be chopping it up into small pieces, for that is the stuff used as filler. The instrument they use looks like a bow and the string that is tied to the ends of the bow is "twanged" and as it vibrates, it sort of cuts or slices the cotton.

So far as their dress is concerned, just any kind of cotton cloth, colored and generally dirty is wrapped around them. Sometimes however one sees them in what looks like a blouse and white duck pants. And now and then a jacket is added to the loin cloth to create a rather incongruous sight. Only a handful of natives wear shoes, and still less, shoes and stockings. Those who do, generally speak English fairly well, and several Indians who work right here on the Base are rather well educated. Thru them I've been able to pick up a little "local color."

As for the other shops in town, except for the ware they display, they are almost alike. However here and there may be found a well educated Indian, in European dress. It is these few, here and elsewhere, in India who are India's hope for the future. But if this town is any indication of what there is to be found in this country, the task of bringing a decent life to its people is just about insurmountable.

Walter Formigli and Joe Molina, two of this Basha's four occupants have been to Calcutta, and they tell me that it is quite a city. Now I look forward to being able to get a day off and ride there, to nose around a bit. But I don't really count on it, tho it's a short ride and trips there are frequent.

When we were in, we saw among the thousands only 3 women and two were veiled. They must have been Brahmins. My Indian "friend" here on the base tells me that women are discouraged from showing themselves since 3 or 4 of them were, as he put it, "snatched away" by soldiers. "Indian Soldiers." But since the town is off limits after six o'clock, at nite, he says they come out now and then in the evening. Back home sometimes it isn't safe for an unescorted woman at nite, here in India, the opposite is true.

I'm tired now, and shall say goodnite, sweetheart. I'm smoking my pipe again and I shall try it again soon. No doubt I'll see your face in the smoke rings I try to blow as I sit outside and gaze upon a really starlit sky. I love you so very dearly. Millions of kisses for you and Robert. You are all I love,

Always and Forever,

CHICK

❖

Chapter 11

## I HAVE NEVER LEFT YOUR SIDE                    1944

For fourteen months after Chick left Bowman Field for overseas duty, we each led two lives. Foremost was the life within the letters; we wrote every day, usually relating normal and happy moments, visiting with each other as though no distance existed. Second was living the days of separation.

Construction, halted for the duration of the war, had created a major apartment crunch. My in-laws also had a three-room apartment and offered to take me there. My parents shrugged off their invitation and assumed I would come back "home." Since no one had more room than the other, going home made the most sense for me.

My parents immediately began to rearrange their apartment to accommodate my needs. Three handsome mahogany pieces in the bedroom were shuffled around to make room for the single bed for Robert. His baby chest of drawers and toy chest were squeezed in on either side of the double bed. My mother cleared a deep roomy drawer in the dresser for my things and found a bit more space in the armoire as well. Everyone's hanging clothes were scrunched into the one bedroom closet, and all the coats, jackets, suits and such went into the only other closet in the front hall. Any piece of furniture with legs became a storage center. Boxes of out-of-season clothes, or infrequently used items were stashed under the bed, dresser, armoire, tables in the living room or china closet in the foyer. My mother then announced that I was to sleep in the bedroom and she and my father would use the pull-out sofa bed in the living room. I was appalled.

"Absolutely not," I said. The sofa bed was uncomfortable and I considered it unreasonable for them to give up their wonderful double bed. I wanted to move Robert's bed into the living room if necessary.

"I don't want to spoil my living room," my mother said. "It won't kill us to sleep here; after all you and Chick did." She wanted people to be able to visit without seeing the clutter. "Robert's bed stays in the bedroom and you have to sleep there with him." When I threatened to move in with my in-laws, she replied, "Forget it, it won't be better there!" My father added his assurances. The living room had French doors which would afford them some privacy, and he didn't mind the sofa bed. There was no bucking their decision. My mother required only one thing. Toys, books, crayons, etc. could be underfoot all day, but in the evening, everything had to be picked up and stashed somewhere. Then, with the clutter tucked away, she could enjoy relatively neat surroundings, and visitors could come visit. We'd manage.

My daily life revolved around caring for Robert and coping with two sets of grandparents. Robert was the most fun. Intrigued by our addiction to reading newspapers, he would sit and mimic my mother and myself by holding a newspaper just as we did, moving his head from left to right. Then with a mischievous look, he'd peek around the paper and laugh as if to say, "I can play this silly game too." Soon he was pointing to the large headline letters on the page asking, "What's 'at?" My mother or I would answer, "That's an L" or

*December 1944*
*Robert reading the newspaper.    Robert reading a letter from his dad.*

"That's an R," or whatever. We were both astonished at his interest. Before long we began to turn the game around. I would point and ask, "What's that?" and sure enough he could recognize the letters and name them.

I sent photo's of this in lengthy letters to amuse Chick, describing how the newspaper game was leading Robert to the beginnings of reading.

Grandparents were quite another thing. I tried to visit Chick's parents once a week, usually on Sunday. Getting to their home was a chore. Though the distance was only about two miles, it could take almost an hour to make the trip without a car. I would take a trolley part way and transfer to a bus to complete the trip. That meant waiting endlessly on cold and windy street corners for each part of the trip. With a two-year-old in tow, it was often impossible. The weather turned unusually cold in December, and January of 1945 was brutal.

There were six or seven snow storms that month, including a blizzard on the 16th of January, reported as the worst since the Blizzard of 1888. Temperatures dropped well below zero and stayed there. Two trans-ocean flying boats were ice-blocked for three weeks. Workers couldn't get to their jobs. Subways were delayed, their switches and car doors frozen. LaGuardia airport canceled flights many times. It seemed like the freezing rain, ice and snow would never end. Since I did not have money for cab rides, all this interfered significantly with visiting during these months.

The telephone came to the rescue and I called often. They received about one letter a week from Chick, but they were unhappy and lonesome. I tried to supplement what they heard by reading from my letters. The only respite from their anxiety came when I was able to bring Robert and visit. They almost never came to me. "It's not the same thing," they said. When I pressed them to come visit until the weather improved, they said it was too cold for them as well.

I was a bit miffed at their attitude, but my mother and father were enraged.

"Do they really expect you to drag Robert out on such a day?" Their anger and support comforted me. It was helpful for them to vent their anger through me. I would agree with their comments, but asked them not to berate Beckie or Sam when they talked together. For the most part I saw myself as a buffer between both sets of in-laws. Chick's parents harbored some envy because my parents could see their grandson daily. Sam would ask me to move in with them. "Why not?" he would ask. "We'll take better care of you. Come, you'll see." My parents, on the other hand, did not view their circumstance as enviable. Seeing their grandson daily was both a pleasure and a trial. They were certainly inconvenienced by the bulging apartment and new sleeping arrangements, but if I moved to my in-laws (who did not have more space) that would have been a slap in the face. Negotiating between the two families could be frustrating and I was determined to keep cool and come through this period with as little damage as possible to both relationships.


Chick's daily life was the cruel and brutal Asian war, but he almost never complained. He was committed to keeping those of us at home confident that he was safe, that all would end well, and we would have our life together. Many of the horrors I was to learn about only in military history accounts, and the books I have mentioned.

Classification was dull and heartbreaking work at the same time. Keeping records of flights, seeing planes take off around the clock, knowing each day that some would not return, yet more were needed, was numbing. Numbers meant men, and their lives were always on the line.

The letters were a life line to another world for us both, and for Chick, the writing was the perfect escape. His innate optimism and ability to lose himself in dreams of love reached beyond the endless days of boredom and frustration. They were the key that helped him keep his sights on tomorrow, another day closer to the longed for day to come. He moved his spirit and self onto the page using poetry, once again, to release emotion.


Our letter-lives moved in slow motion. A letter traveled fourteen days one way and the reply fourteen days back; twenty-eight days at best before questions were answered or conversations completed. During these twenty-eight day intervals we moved robot like, sus-

pended in an emotionless existence. We wrote to fend off the emptiness, to sustain hope, to affirm love, to get through the days. We strove
to express the agreeable events in our lives, avoiding anything that
might cause anxiety for the other. Occasionally, a disagreement would
erupt but the lapse of twenty-eight days awaiting a response resolved
anger. Life was strangely jumbled, the past becoming present as
letters caught up with the days.

The poems, here interspersed, started to appear soon after his
arrival in Sylhet, India, bringing magic into my life. They pushed
every button — love, tears, laughter, longing, wonder and so much
hope.

❖

"He is gone," they say, over oceans blue
And trackless desert wastes; and strange places
Have caught his eye in passing. It is true
They sent me away, to be among strange faces.

Yet I have never left your side. Do you hear
The murmurings of leaves as they dance
Among the trees? It is I, whispering; near.

"Half a world away, in a foreign land,
In a strange clime, there midst endless days
He sits," That's what they say. With a wave of my hand
I said "Goodbye." But I'm with you still in so many ways.

Has a song delighted you and filled your heart
With Love? Has a cool breeze caressed you?
It is I, kissing you. We are not apart!

These words say so inadequately what I feel. No bard of old could ever capture the love I have for you, the longings I feel and put them to words. How can I. But if your heart is listening, my heart will tell it. Someday we'll be together, living it. You are all I love. Always and forever, I love you, Ros, I love you so much.

CHICK

Assam, India
15 Dec 44

Darling,

I guess I ought to be mad enough to spit nails and grind up infant babies, but I feel too good for all that! The reason for all of this is, you guessed, no letter from you. Only the fact that one of these days, your mail will catch up to me makes me feel better.. The thought of reading a big batch of letters like the first one I got keeps me on an even keel.

I showered again and then wended my way to the mess hall. No need to tell you that I approached it with trepidation and grave misgivings. After all, it was late and the fate of the tail-enders on an army chow line is universally known. They are simply lucky to get anything to eat. And here they run out of bread and this and that in the middle of the line at times. But lo and behold—when Walter and I and two others came up — they had lots of home-fried potatoes and scrambled eggs, coffee, and bread for us. And this time the eggs were freshly made and really delicious.. The four of us just loaded up and ate leisurely and toward the end of the repast, we entered upon an interesting discussion about nothing at all. Then for our stroll back and a few glances at a brilliant star studded sky. A few moments of relaxation and now a visit with you.

The boys finally got on the ball and visited the PX and now we have an adequate supply of Tootsie Rolls and crackers. That is, if another shipment arrives in two or three weeks. If not, why then we'll be slightly inconvenienced.

That settled, our next major campaign is to be waged against our old friends "The Rats." Up to now, whenever the "High Command" met in informal session, only make-shift suggestions were advanced. One or two were carried out. The situation reached a head when some of the boys went to bed but kept their carbines, 45 cal. revolvers handy, and they were solemn in their determination to use them. A true account of the "Rats" success in devastating our belongings would bring tears to your eyes. They have variously gorged themselves on candy, uniforms, flying jackets, stationery, books, duffel bags, etc. My own losses have been slight — one handkerchief ruined and two large holes nibbled out of a pair of shorts. Other's losses have been more grievous. Incidentally, note the ridge atop the pages of this letter. That's where the mice nibbled the glue that serves to keep the pages of this pad together.

One night one of us took a Tootsie Roll and cut it into little pieces. Then he broke a bottle and ground it into little pieces. Then he pounded it further until he almost had powdered glass. It was a tasty dish, guaranteed to rip any human's intestines. Properly placed around the Basha, we thought it would do the trick. We hit the hay and soon we heard the "patter of little feet."

Well, the next morning, the candy was gone and we congratulated ourselves. But too soon. The next nite it

109

seemed as tho not only he, but all his relatives came. Not only didn't it kill him, the little bastard loved the stuff. One of the boys swears that the rat left a note for him on the writing table saying that his feelings were hurt at finding no delicacies after he brought some friends to dinner. And then "just for laughs" the Rat ate chunks out of the guy's canteen cover.

So tonite, seated in council, it was decided to take stern measures. Joseph was delegated to secure rat poison from the orderly room. That done, Bennie, Walter and I proceeded to sprinkle it liberally over some candy and sweet crackers. The boys are now busily engaged placing the stuff in every nook and cranny.

Bets are now being laid on the efficacy of this treatment. Some are convinced that it will work, others are unimpressed. I'm not so sure that it will. After all, a rat smart enough to write a note is clever enough to avoid poison. Then again, maybe he's built up an immunity against the stuff. If this doesn't work, then I am prepared to appeal to the Rat and try to convince him of the justice of the Allied cause and then enlist him in our aid. If he and his friends could be persuaded to bring their full weight to bear against the Japs, why then half the battle here will be won. But we shall see. A communiqué from this Headquarters will be forthcoming in the morning.

I did get a letter today from Etty and among other things she tells of the home she bought. I'll bet it's a beauty. I shall make every effort to write her in the morning.

The nites and mornings seem to have gotten colder. That's all right with me. As long as it doesn't get colder than three blankets worth. I'm using two now.

More and more, I long to be near you to tell you again of my love for you. How much I think and dream of you and one of these days I shall do so, for pages and pages and the censor, whoever it may be, will surely get an "eyeful."

I love you so dearly and so very, very much. You are all my life. Won't you stay well and happy and take care of yourself. Millions of kisses for you and Rob.

> All my love,
> Forever
> CHICK

ODE TO THE POSTMASTER-GENERAL
OR HOW ARE THESE FOR THOUGHTS, BABY,
WHILE WAITING FOR ATC TO DELIVER OUR MAIL,
WHILE SWEATING IT OUT IN THE CBI

Earlier this day, the boys all said,
"There's mail tonite, there's got to be,
Before I start those dreams in bed,
I'll have read six letters addressed to me."

We met again about ten to five
and Paul smiled and said "My gal
Has sent sugar reports to keep me alive
And to buck up that old morale."

Nick smiled and hopped around like mad,
"I know I'll soon be feasting my eyes,
On many long letters and I'll be glad,
And not be as blue as those skies."

Chick reared up and said, "he knew
That there should be mail to spare,
Letters and packages would all come thru
For everyone here to share!"

And that young Texan, with the southern drawl,
Leaned back and said, "Why shore,
If I don't get any, I'll sure as hell bawl,
I must be gettin' three or four."

Steward came up and rubbed his hands
And swore it was bound to break.
His veins stood out iron bands
When he thought of the haul he'd make.

 It's about time, I got a letter
From the gal in old San Fran,"
Said Earl who surely should know better
Than to think that he was her man,

So we stood around with spirits high
And hearts full of anticipation,
When the mail clerk whispered with a sigh
There's NO Mail for This Station

So now we're all sweating, still,
But we know we're licked you see,
For it's mail we're sweating and always will,
As long as it's carried by ATC
              Finis…

There it is, and that's about the size of it. This is really a Damn Tough War!!

Assam, India
20 Dec 44

Darling,

Just as I started this, the strains of a very old song came out of the radio. Truthfully, for years the ghost of it would occasionally flit thru my mind but it would never quite jell. The name is — "The Folks Who Live on the Hill". I heard it sung by Irene Dunne a long time ago, in a picture, whose name I've long forgotten. Imagine hearing it after so many years, in of all places — Hell's Half Acre, Assam, India.

We had quite a fine time tonite. For a long time I decided that there must be a way to "beat the Racket," or in other words, to add to our G.I. diet, things that sane soldiers consider to be impossible to get here. For a while I thought about it and looked around and asked questions. Well, I won't write you the details now, but I treated the boys to a royal repast tonite. Can you imagine the looks of amazement on their faces when they saw, and then ate, real, live, crispy, crunchy Post Toasties, (made in USA)? With milk and sugar too? They swooned and jabbered wildly. For a while I thought they'd be candidates for a Section VIII. Then they ate and ate and ate.

When they finished, I shoved a canteen cup full of delicious, hot, steaming cocoa (Bakers) and sweet crackers in front of them. Ho, ho! You should have been around. The look of complete pleasure was reward enough for the trouble I went to. And later at nite, I pulled out the piece de resistance, a tin of herring and lobster paste! And that spread on small pretzels, together with "cheddar cheese" made remarkably delicious canapes of hor's d'oevres, or as we in the 15th call them, Hawz Dawvrez! These we drowned in cans of beer and a wonderful time was had by all.

Now what does this prove? Only that "many a rose is born to blush unseen" or that only a guy who spends some time looking under bushes, can find things of which dreams are made. Tomorrow early, ye scribe is to set out on another expedition to see if the larder can be kept well stocked. This evening was so very successful that we plan to supplement our diet often with the above. Much as I'd like to share our good fortune with others in the squadron, there just isn't enough to go around. So we shall have to make an effort to keep the source of my supply a "Top Secret." You needn't worry, (nor you either, censor) all of this is above board and legal, paid for with good Indian rupees.

So you see, that altho this was another "mailless day" for us, it wasn't too bad. But I'd gladly have forgone all the fun for a few letters from you. All the effort in doing these crazy things serves only to keep me from going completely whacky.

I think of you constantly and dream of starting back home to you. Someone once wrote, "How do I love you, let me count the ways." For me to count them is well nigh impossible. It would take years and a steady torrent of words to describe you and the reasons for my love. And in addition I love you too, for love's sake!

Take extra good care of yourself, Sweetheart. Stay well and happy. You and Robert are all my life and all I love,

Always and Forever.
CHICK

❖

And then the best birthday gift arrived - this poem dated 28 Dec. 44, Assam, India.

❖

My Dearest Darling Ros,

Ask not why my eyes are languid,
And attention so hard to hold;
There are days for smiling
There are nights when the heart
     is cold.
So, Madonna, on this nite of your
     birthday
When joy is large enough to share
Can I now play the part of Pagliacci
when I am so far from there?

Yet, closed eyes bring to light your image
So charming, so lovely, so fair
Darling, how but to be happy?
Forgetting this cruel world of care?

So see now, my heart is lighter
When your very dear face I behold
Madonna, there are days for smiling,
But tonite, the heart is not cold.

Remembrance of past pleasures
              between us,
Serves to brighten my skies,
Madonna, now see how your image
Brings the sparkle of love to my eyes.
And now tho the world is between us,
And of presents my cupboard is bare
Take my love and my heart for your
              own dear
And best wishes for a life, free from care!

Many many happy returns of the day, dearest. I received a gift too, in the form of two letters from you, nos. 22 and 24. Thanks a great deal for the air mail stamps. Until further notice, I don't think you ought to send any more for they are more readily available than formerly. Now that you've sent the trunks and another "small gift" I am eagerly awaiting their arrival. You do know that I bought a fountain pen. If a new one hasn't already been bought for me, please discourage my Aunt from doing so. I think I'll be able to manage with this one very well.......

Chapter 12


# A JOB AND DREAMS                                    1945

Once the first letters arrived from Sylhet, India and I knew Chick was well, I began to review the options open to me. Getting a job was the most appealing. I did not consult with my family or Chick's, but once my parents heard I was contemplating work, they had no qualms about letting me know just how they felt. Simply put — if you wanted to work you didn't have children; if you had children you stayed home and looked after them. For once they all agreed but it was not helpful. I decided to move ahead none the less.

If I could place Robert in a nursery school, I would look for work. That was not as easy as it sounded. Private schools were too expensive. I tried looking around for subsidized child care nearby, but no luck. I was not angry that my mother did not offer to care for Robert so that I might work. All through my growing up years, she had always insisted on doing every work detail in the house. At no time would she allow me to wash the dishes, cook, change the beds or vacuum. She would not make a fuss if I helped clear the table or dried some dishes. But that was it! She was the mother, that was her job. I was not her servant.

"You'll do enough of that in your life," she said then. "Just go to school." Now it was, "Just take care of Robert."

Baby sitting on occasion was O.K. but I could not add regular, daily care-giving to her day. It was never an option.

My mother-in-law could not be helpful either. She was a sedentary person who would be bowled over by a child as active as Robert. Besides, she had developed angina and could not stand on her feet or walk for any length of time.

One thing I could do was look for a job in a nursery school where I would be willing to work for less money if they would place Robert in a class.

In late December I spotted a nursery-school ad for an assistant teacher who could play the piano. I had taken piano lessons for years and could read new music quickly and easily. Just thinking about it made my fingers tingle. I called for an appointment.

My mother had sewn some lovely outfits for me. On the appointed day, I chose something appropriate to wear, applied some makeup carefully, combed my hair back (for that mature look), dropped Robert off with a friend, and left for the job interview.

As I approached the small private school, I thought my pounding heart would surely give me away. The gabled red brick building sat neatly on a small lot and I could see some jungle gym and slide equipment in the fenced yard. Looks good, I thought, while stopping to take one long, deep breath to still the butterflies. As I rang the bell, I told myself, "It's just an interview, not the end of the world."

Rosalind - That mature look.

An attractive, dark haired woman greeted me, introducing herself as the director; the natural exchange of names and weather comments put me at ease. The school was empty since the Christmas vacation had already begun. Across the desk, I saw a mature, confident, worldly, well put together woman, probably in her forties — all the things I hoped I could become someday. After a very brief discussion about my background courses in early childhood education, she moved on to question me, at some length, about my piano abilities. It became clear that this was an important requirement for the job. My response must have convinced her it was worth a gamble. As for Robert, if he could keep up with the two-to-three-year-old class, there would be no problem. I was to be the assistant teacher with the four-to-five-year-old group. Then handing me some music to take home and review, she wished me a happy holiday and asked me to start right after the New Year.

My first interview, my first job and a perfect solution. I was ecstatic. I danced all the way home exhilarated by my success, yet tempered by some trepidation that I might not live up to expectations. Little did I know how imperfect it could be.

There was no round of applause when the family heard the news. My mother was wary and my father asked, "Why do you have to work?"

"I don't have to," I said. "I want to."

Sam took it all personally. Inferring that my parents were not providing enough for me, he said, "Come here, let me take care of you." He thought wives did not go to work unless they were destitute. Besides, wouldn't Chick be upset to learn I had to work? Then the nub of his problem spilled out — it would demean him if I worked. What would his friends think? I laughed and told him teasingly that he was old fashioned. I assured him that I was not destitute, and that Chick did not mind at all. Shaking his head, he threw his hands up, and wondered aloud what the world was coming to. He wasn't angry, just puzzled. Beckie only listened. They were caring parents who needed time to accept the changing world swirling around them.

Getting through the holiday season was most difficult, but I had something to keep me busy. I would have to spend some time practicing the music. I had studied Chopin, Bach and Mendelssohn, but that was not going to help me much with the skipping, marching, jumping, lumbering (make like an elephant) rhythms. I understood what was needed for the children's music periods and with a bit of practice I could learn these simple notes and songs. But to do them well, I would have to develop creative sets of movement to suit the activities and I had no experience with anything like that. I had never improvised on the piano and did not feel I could segue from one rhythm to another. Robert became my little guinea pig. I would play, he would sway back and forth but without other children to watch and mimic he always ended up on the piano bench wanting to play the keys instead.

I visited with friends and tried to keep my loneliness from showing. Robert talked about going to school and seemed very excited about it, but my mother was still not enamored of the plan. At first she was wary and noncommittal. We both knew I would have to get Robert up, fed, and bundled up by 8:30 in the morning in order to be at work by 9:00. Once the weather turned colder she began to view the morning rush as a form of torture for her grandson. Soon she was arguing against my working. I chose to be silent. I wanted to prevent a full blown argument but the silence enraged her and made her sullen. It was not the happiest December and I would not share these domestic squabbles in my letters to Chick. I couldn't wait for the New Year to begin along with my job, thinking once we got going, my mother would change her mind.

The first day of school, Robert was hesitant about being left in a class without me, but all the toys and activity quickly diverted his attention. Soon he was mingling with the group and I could move on to meet the teacher with whom I would work. Ms B. Was short and stout; her straight hair cropped short and scraggly, give her a rumpled look. Overall she appeared old fashioned. But, within minutes, it became clear that she was a super teacher. She brought the class to order easily and with a planned surprise, engaged their interest. She handed me her plans for the day and as I gathered the cutting and coloring things needed, I thought, "Oh yes, I am going to enjoy working with her." I set about organizing the tasks so that the children could begin and found that I was skillful in working with the children. I thoroughly enjoyed analyzing the different personalities, encouraging shy ones with a little warmth or praise, helping unruly ones find something of interest to distract them. On the other hand, my piano skills were still rusty and though I was not comfortable ad-libbing with the music as needed, I hoped to remedy that in time. With each passing day I learned more about early childhood education and I could see that Robert was benefiting as well. At home he would offer to share his cookies with us or a friend. Of course, he demanded we reciprocate. He would often say "thank you" now, without prodding, although he balked at saying "please." He was learning to get along well with other children, and having fun doing it. I was delighted.

The teaching was great, but events soon conspired to muck up the whole plan. The weather was most uncooperative. January came in like an elephant swinging its trunk in a glass factory. On the second day, wind and rainstorms disrupted transportation; plants were closed and night shifts canceled. By the tenth, the weather bureau reported the coldest day ever recorded. Innumerable snowfalls and below zero days became the norm. When the worst blizzard since 1888 hit, Robert came down with a sore throat, cold and temperature of 103°, something I should have anticipated. Without any back-up baby sitting arrangements at hand, the "jig was up." Of course, I would stay home to care for Robert but the school needed me every day. I had enjoyed the work for three and one half weeks but my only option now was to leave.

As I mulled over the events of the month, the January freeze turned out in some perverse way, to be a boon. It brought an end to the growing tensions at home. The original accommodating spirit in the house had begun to deteriorate. Since my mother never tired of berating me for putting my job before my child, it put a strain on everyone. My father, gentle and soft spoken, often felt constrained to come to my defense. With Robert ill, we had all the ingredients for an explosion. Now with my working days behind me, my mother relaxed. After an "I told you so" or two, she started to smile again and my father no longer had to run interference to soften her regular caustic comments. Robert recovered quickly and my mother volunteered to look after him evenings and even afternoons if I wanted to go out. It was an offer I would not refuse. I needed the freedom and she needed a way to say she was sorry for having given me a very hard time.

I could not look to Chick for comfort in the trying days; instead I could write him that all was well and that my mother had become most amenable when I gave up working. Of course I could write with the deepest longing of how I missed him and wanted him home just as he continued to write me.

Assam Province India

4 Jan

Dearest Darling Rosalind,

For the life of me, I can't recall when I wrote you last. I know it's been several days, but tho I've racked my brains, I can't hang my hat on any particular day. The reason for not writing may not be entirely adequate, but here it is! We've moved! The whole damn outfit, just like that! But in terms of miles traversed and time taken to do so, it's hardly worth mentioning. As you can see, we're still in the same Indian Province, or if not, just inside the neighboring one. We are a bit closer to Calcutta but so far as my chances of getting there are concerned, I might just as well be in China, or Timbuctoo!

But the move cost mightily in terms of spent effort and lost sleep, etc. To begin with, we knew for several days that we were leaving. We even knew where! But when? Several days passed and the eventual counter rumor started; "We weren't going!" And just as that one reached a high spot and gathered more momentum, at 7:00 PM several days ago, we were told to have our bags fully packed, out in front of the "Basha" at 8:00 PM, so that they could be loaded on the trucks and taken to the planes. What bedlam. Ho!ho! What a mad rush! Remember now, one of the boys in our Basha was away at another base, in the hospital (it developed, for no good reason at all) having a high time, so Walter and I not only had our own things to pack, but his stuff also.

I suppose we ought to be accustomed to moving, at this stage of the game, but I guess we never shall. Finally we had our bags crammed full. In addition to some of the things we picked up since arrival, they also issued folding cots to us. You recall the kind the boys at Lakeview had? We were certainly loaded down. As usual, the trucks which were to take the bags were only a figment of someone's imagination. We were now to get our bags to the planes assigned to take all the Squadron's luggage. Since we lived at the end of the company street, the truck was always fully loaded before it got to us. So we catnapped while waiting for it.

At long last, Walter and I boarded it, the first time at about 11:15 PM. It was a tough job but we got our bags on board. Then we had to head back for another trip, for we had more baggage than could be handled in just one trip! At 1:15 AM we were pretty well set! We fell asleep and were rudely awakened at 4:00 AM and groping blindly in the "Stygian Darkness." We dressed hurriedly and packed our bed-clothes etc. Again we waited. Since Walter had to get out to preflight his plane, he managed to "mooch" a ride with some kind Samaritan. However, I was left at the church. After a lapse of two hrs., I finally made it! But my plane went on without me. Fortunately, I got a ride on a

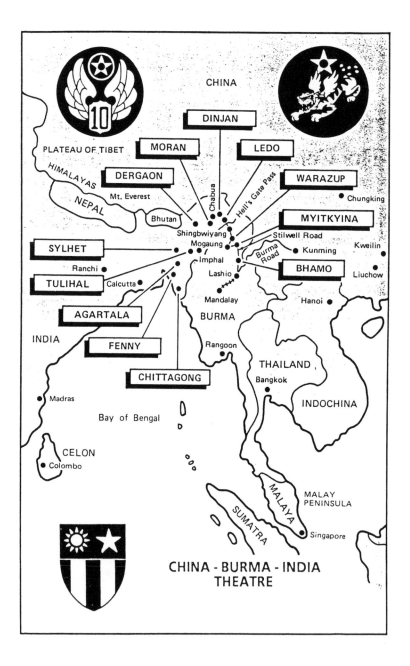

CHINA

PLATEAU OF TIBET

HIMALAYAS

NEPAL

Mt. Everest

Bhutan

**DINJAN**

**MORAN**

**LEDO**

**DERGAON**

Chabua

Hell's Gate Pass

**WARAZUP**

Chungking

Shingbwiyang

Stilwell Road

**MYITKYINA**

Kweilin

**SYLHET**

Mogaung

Imphal

Burma Road

Kunming

**BHAMO**

Liuchow

Ranchi

Lashio

**TULIHAL**

Calcutta

Mandalay

Hanoi

**AGARTALA**

BURMA

INDIA

**FENNY**

Rangoon

**CHITTAGONG**

THAILAND

Bangkok

Madras

INDOCHINA

Bay of Bengal

CELON

Colombo

MALAY PENINSULA

MALAYA

SUMATRA

Singapore

CHINA - BURMA - INDIA
THEATRE

plane whose purpose was to pick stragglers up. A short ride, 32 minutes, and I stepped out to look around at my new home.

I'd like to describe it fully but honestly, I don't know a hell of a lot about it. It seems much larger, more beautiful. Our company area certainly is a vast improvement over the old one. Here, there is a fairly good shower room. The latrines are of the "slit trench" variety with some embellishments. Thus far we've been eating "C" rations, heating them and coffee, over hastily built fireplaces. They are now taking a lot of time and a great deal of pain in setting up the Mess Hall. Rumor has it that it will really be "on the beam."

The Bashas this time are much larger, and we were *assigned* beds therein. Now I find myself with about 19 other men, all doing a variety of clerical tasks! That old gang is really split up, and as a consequence Walter and I make appointments to meet and talk things over. I run into the others now and then, during the day. The natives around are pretty much the same. All of them seem to be beasts of burden in human form. There is a fairly large town about 6 miles away, and in the other direction, about 1 ½ miles away may be found a "Bazaar" or "Market." One of these days, I'll make a quick trip to see for myself what it's all about.

You can tell Bernie that the wallet was made in Calcutta, and if any are available, I'll send some home. I have thought of getting some Indian jewelry here, and again if any there be, I'll try to get some!

Your birthday card came today, together with no.'s 25 and 26. I got no. 27 four days ago, and was surprised as hell to find that it was mailed on the 19th. It got to me on the 31st. Now we're current again. Yesterday I got the clippings but I haven't had a chance to read one of them yet. But I'm exceedingly grateful for them!

No need to tell you how nostalgic the card caused me to feel. Tho I haven't been able to write in the last three days I've been thinking of you constantly. I love you so very dearly, so very much. You are all I love!

In the past two days I've gotten letters from Sol from Hawaii, and Larry in England. I have a great deal of writing to do to catch up with my correspondence. I haven't written Mom too, in 4 days. Please explain why and reassure her as to my well-being! I'll write them tomorrow. Millions of kisses to you and Rob. I'm eagerly awaiting the trunks and the wallet you sent. Love,

Always and Forever<br>CHICK

P.S. Please note, my address is the same as the old one, even tho we've moved!!

"DAYDREAMS, OR THOUGHTS ONE NITE WHILE BLOWING SMOKE RINGS TOWARD YOUR PICTURE BABY WHILE SWEATING IT OUT IN THE CBI"!!

I

What dreams are these
Castles rising midst a summer glen
Galleons, that sail the seven seas
A man, stalking where men are men?

II

Out of "Ivanhoe" or "Richard the Great"
Lion-hearted am I, and fair
As Paris (so fortunate)whose very fate
It was, the love of Helen to share?

III

Dreams of youth, since gone by
When first I turned the pages of books
That spurred the mind to dream and sigh
At thoughts of De Milo and her fabulous looks.

IV

Now, years past, when life is real
And every day, is not to be wasted
What are these keen thoughts I feel
Of life, to be lived, of a future, only tasted?

V

Dreams are of you, and I explore
The future by your side at every turn.
No longer the "Idols" of "Forgotten Lore"
Cause the flames of adventure and love to burn.

VI

With you, life is living, as it's meant to be
Happily, each day fanning love anew,
Together, no birds are half so free
As I am, with my Love for you!

❖

As Chick had written, in early January 1945, the 4th Combat Cargo Group moved to Agartala, India. The war, real and ugly, raged throughout Burma. Monsoon rains flooded the landing strips creating new dangers for pilots and soldiers. While nearby Japanese held villages were still burning from bombings and strafing by the P-47's and RAF spitfires, air strips were hastily built by army engineers. The roads too were improved as the British advanced with increasing speed.

On January 31, 1945, in order to keep up with the British and Indian fighting units the 4th Group was ordered to move once again, this time to Chittagong, a large seaport city on the coast of the Bay of Bengal, bordering Burma.

Operations never stopped during their move. The 4th Combat Cargo Group went on a 24-hour, round-the-clock flying schedule. Each new advance meant another open airstrip to be supplied and serviced by the group. Ondaw, a major supply point, was the first airfield where the 4th experienced the jarring blows of battle. The pilots could see the Japanese artillery firing from the hills along the banks of the river. Some were exploding on the landing strip. The British fought hard but it took several weeks to clear the enemy's guns from the hills along the Irrawaddy.

More and more, Chick turned to poetry and dreams to escape his hateful world and his loneliness. Sometimes I kept a letter, sometimes only the poems in the letters.

❖

...Seated, looking out at a cloudy Burma sky. The moon keeps running in behind the big clouds carrying on a flirtation with the stars. It's lovely and slightly cool. Too damn nice to hit the sack. But I'm tired now, and I must.

By the Irrawaddy waters
Ringed by mountains high
I stand and watch the lazy clouds
Think of you and sigh.

God how lovely, oh how sweet
Is your image that I see
And I wish upon the star so bright
Just a hope for you and me.

A hope for you to withstand care
For me to carry my head so high
A wish that our love will burn so bright
And never, ever, die.

I love you, adorable, lovable Ros. You are all I dream of, think of, and love. Every day brings new longings and desires and yet too, it brings us closer. I love you so, how can I ever tell you of it. Will our lifetime together be enough?

**CHICK**

Assam, India
6 Jan. 1945

Dearest Darling Rosalind,

What do you know? It rained all day and all last nite, and those who know, say that it wasn't a drop in the bucket compared with what happens in this part of the world from

June to October. Well, if they're correct, and I'm still in this neighborhood then, I'll sure as hell need those bathing trunks you sent, for anything more than this is "swimming weather."

Since I volunteered to work all night, last night, I was off today and finally got several things done that needed doing badly. In as much as I hadn't unpacked my bags since we left the States, I did that first. Then I rearranged everything so that I'd know exactly where it could be found. After that I made a bundle up for the native laundry man, and saw it safely on its way to be washed. I wrote several letters and hit the sack for a few hrs. In the afternoon, despite the rain, I went to the village. This is more truly an Indian village, in that it's smaller than the one near our previous base; and thus what there is to see, is more apparent. Their homes are only ramshackle bamboo thatched bashas, small, and for the most part windowless. The adults work in the fields, (rice paddies) and the youngsters, hordes of them, are to be seen playing in the courtyards. They are scantily dressed and those who appear to be but 2 years old or so, wear no clothes at all. Their coloring seems to be darker than those natives we left behind, but that may be only because it was a very cloudy day, (when it wasn't raining).

The market place is only about the size of a city block, with what is probably the usual stalls and wares displayed in them. Since it rained a good deal of the time I was there, it was merely an exploratory visit and so I did no serious looking for souvenirs. But from what I did gather, if I'm to get anything worthwhile here, it will have to be bought in the other, larger town about 8 miles from the base!

As I had a jagged rip in my flight jacket, I sought out a tailor to mend it. As I waited while he plied his trade, I struck up a conversation with one of his Indian friends. This fellow spoke English quite well; and as luck would have it, he turned out to be the president of what seems to be the Local Town Board! I was really surprised to hear him speak of Roosevelt as a "great man," and for him to recall Dewey as his opponent in the recent elections! I was under the impression that no one anywhere would remember Tom Dewey! We spoke for a while of Ghandi ( or Gandhi) and Nehru and Hinnah, and of the Indian's needs and hopes. During my stay, I introduced him to Yank cigarettes and chewing gum, and to pictures of you and Robert! He had never seen or chewed gum before and it was quite an experience for me to explain to him what it was all about. We discussed methods of farming here, and he was exceedingly anxious to hear of American mechanized farming methods.

And after about an hour and a half I left him with the promise that I would return with pictures of a large American building, or a panoramic shot of a city. I hope to be able to cut some out of some magazines as soon as I can get them. Then I strolled thru the rain, with an English soldier who has been here 2 ½ years and overseas for 3 ½ yrs. The poor bastard expects to get home sometime in July. If I thought I'd be here that long, I'd go mad! Stark Raving Mad, at that! Then a jeep came along, and back to camp I came.

Then came chow time and back to work, for I'm working again tonite! Matter of fact, the work remains interesting and so far, so good.

The food here is better than it was when we left the other place, even tho it is the same cooks who prepare it. But it started off well there also, so we are waiting to see if it will stay this way. All in all, this base is preferable to the other and I hope to stay here for several months at least. But since we are so "mobile", we can pick up and go most any time.

No mail for the last several days, no letter more recent than the one dated 18 Dec. That is because the "mail shuttle" didn't fly again today due to the weather. But it is fine tonite and tomorrow promises to be sunny again. Then I expect to be reading your letters most of the nite.

It's coming round to my birthday again. Just another day here, as all of them are. But one day, when this is over, we'll make up for all the deficiencies this war has caused us. You and Robert are constantly before me and I love you more than ever. You are all my life, all my love! Stay well and take care of yourself. Best regards to your folks and the "gang." Tell Bernie and Morris, that they'll never believe the "tales of splendor" I shall tell, when I return.

As ever,

CHICK

## ODE TO THE FAIR MAIDEN LOOKING
## OUT OF THE WINDOW AT THE
## RAGING BLIZZARD OF FEBRUARY 8, 1945

"So it's cold and dreary and snowing
and the wind takes your breath away,
Leaving you chilled to the marrow
To spend a perfectly miserable day.
May I send you a warm zephyr breeze,
With the sun in a sky of blue
And this thought "You are all I care for,"
With this promise, "My love is true."

The days merge into weeks and they in turn, into months. Ever slowly the sands of time run out. So be it! Never before have I wished wings on Time, as I do now. And until I come back to you, it shall be ever thus. When you get this, Feb. 14th should be upon us.

There is no day
I love you more.
There is no way
I haven't loved you before.
But if there were
Then I would say
It must be this
Valentine's Day

There it is, an effort unworthy of you or of the way I feel. I could never fully do justice to either. But the day is not too far off, ages tho it will seem, when I shall be able to tell you in millions of ways, how much you mean to me. You are all I love,

Always and Forever

CHICK

P.S. I enclose 2 more pictures for my mother if you see her soon.

22 Feb. 45 India

Dearest Darling Rosalind

I

At dawn, like a Crusader, in years past
Comes the sun blazing, in an azure sky
The peace in my heart seems to welcome the day

II

I strolled to the beach and gazed out to sea
and ships passing by, whistled "View Halloo,"
Wave upon wave rolled up to my feet,
Knelt as I did, when I pledged my heart to you.

III

I stood beneath a blanket of stars,
Near bamboo trees, gently swaying above,
Soft moonlight played on the strings of my heart,
And sang melodies made of our Love!

If anyone doubts that you are in my thoughts constantly, let them be silenced.

Chapter 13

GETTING ON WITH MY LIFE                                    1945

The nightly news on the radio reported freezing weather in
Europe throughout December of 1944 and January, 1945. At
the horrendous Battle of the Bulge, our men fought in heavy snow-
storms and blizzards through endless below-zero days. Allied fliers
encountered bitter cold temperatures recorded as low as 52° below
zero. In New York, as snow continued to blanket the city, two
trans-ocean flying boats, ice-blocked for three weeks, were unable to
leave LaGuardia Field until February 11.

By comparison, our lives were comfortable, and few of us dared
complain about the frigid days. Though heating oil was now rationed,
my warm bathrobe over flannel pajamas was all I needed to keep
warm. Below zero temperatures kept us locked indoors much of the
time, but when the sun came out and the biting winds subsided, we
would bundle up in sweaters, snowsuits, boots, ear muffs, mittens,
hats, and scarves and trundle outdoors for a bit of sledding and fun in
the fresh, glistening snow before it turned to ice. Long walks and
outdoor play were out of the question. At best, we would remain
outside for about 20 minutes and then only if we ran, jumped, kept
moving. Indoors, I spent my time reading and knitting warm sweater
outfits for Robert, intricate patterned ones in bright colors for myself,
and gloves or mittens for everyone. Luckily, I had a most congenial
friend in the building. It was a friendship both unlikely and serendipi-
tous.

One day before Chick left for overseas duty, we bumped into a
young couple and their son as we were leaving the apartment house.
The startled look of recognition on her face as well as Chick's was
quickly followed by smiles and introductions — Julia, Bernie, and
their son Henry. They had moved into the building and now lived one
floor directly below us. As soon as I heard "Julia," I realized that this

was the young woman Chick had dated back in 1938. Beckie had spoken of her several times. Pretty face, nice blue eyes, I thought. What a surprise! Chick and I laughed as we walked away. In a city of seven million, what were the odds for such a coincident? Life can be so fluky we said.

In the days and months that followed, Julia and I often met as we headed for the park. We were on similar schedules. Our boys, the same age, bonded at once. Julia and I enjoyed being together. Relaxed, even tempered, she was as pleased as I with the friendship the boys had found. Since they were the same age, we exchanged anecdotes, shared notes about the best children's books, games and puzzles. She never engaged in the one-upmanship classic among some mothers, and never derided other women or their children. We were compatible. By the time the freezing weather arrived, the boys were accustomed to seeing each other almost every day. When they could not go outdoors, I invited Henry up to our apartment. Since Julia's place was less crowded, Robert often went downstairs. The boys were never at a loss for things to do what with plenty of toys, books and games around. When they argued, they usually preferred to work something out rather than separate.

Locked in our cramped quarters for days at a time, we were all becoming claustrophobic. Julia welcomed visits, and when I felt desperate, I would go down for a short break. When she needed time for herself, I would take Henry upstairs. It was a neat arrangement for each of us as we plowed our way through the first six cold weeks of the new year.

Just as we became resigned to indoor living, for another month at least, the weather changed dramatically. By February 14th, it was suddenly warm. Now we were all sweaty in the same heavy winter outfits that had barely kept us comfortable just days before. We cautiously shed a few layers and for the first time in months filled our lungs with deep, deep breaths of delicious warm air. March arrived redolent of spring, with the warmest day of the year on March 2nd, followed by the warmest March 16th in history — a record 80°. The winter had ended and none too soon.

My mother still walked a fair distance to do the food shopping, and now, rationing had become a way of life. Stamps were issued based on family size and some items were hard to find. Among the things doled out were meat, butter, sugar, coffee, tea, cheese, processed foods, soap, cigarettes, tin, rubber, and gasoline. Sometimes this presented inconveniences. For example, since there was no plastic of any kind in use, rubber boots were essential for the winter snow and spring rain. These were difficult to find. When we wanted to buy a tricycle for Robert we found there were none available. Iron and steel was allocated to the war effort and very little remained for civilian use. Through the grapevine we heard that someone was making bikes out of old pipes. It was a clever idea, and Robert was soon having a good time riding his. Every time I see a sculpture today made of old tools and plumbing supplies, I remember 1945.

My mother would hunt far and wide or stand on lines to get what she wanted. Often she came home tired and cranky without them. On rare occasions she would permit me to go in her place while she stayed with Robert.

Our tempers were on edge; my mother would not give up easily while I was willing to do without hard-to-find items. If she wanted something, she would walk to every store within a three-mile radius. If she was not successful, she would take buses or a subway to scour other neighborhoods.

We disagreed about what we could do without, and what was worth the search. She called me "lazy," I called her "stubborn." Tempers flared, usually over petty things. We needed space.

It was therefore a great relief when, early in March, friends of my folks decided to pool their rationed gas stamps and take two cars to the Catskill mountains to look for a suitable rooming house or bungalow colony for the summer months ahead. They invited my mother to join them.

The weather pundits claimed that a frigid winter would be followed by a blistering summer — a traditional pattern, they said! July and August could be stifling in a New York apartment with no air-conditioning. A place in the country would mean added freedom for us all, and Robert could run and play with little supervision. There would be friends, swimming, space, and cool nights. Even the shopping problems would be easier when shared by the group. I was elated. It would be worth all the money I could spare.

"Don't forget to look for a lake or pool," I instructed as she got ready for the trip. The two cars represented six or more families. I was sure they would succeed.

My father remained at home with Robert and me. There was no room in the cars, and he did not feel it was important for him to go. Come summer, he would become a commuter along with the other men. Husbands would come up on Friday night and leave early Monday morning to get back to work. The women would remain in the country for the summer. I thought this an unfair arrangement and asked my father how he felt about fending for himself all summer. He laughed and joked, saying it made his life easier. He could work late nights at the factory without having to put up with flack from my mother about it. Working late all week made it possible for him to take the week-end off and "come with the guys" for a restful few days away.

"If your mother is happy, I'm happy," he said. "It's really best for both of us."

"How strange," I thought. It could never be best for me if Chick were in the city all week and I wasn't.

Spending a day alone with my dad was a rare treat. His long working days left very little time for quiet conversation. This was the first in a very long time. I learned that his business was doing better. Some government work was beginning to come in; he would be making hats for the Women's Army Corps Service (WACS). Since things were looking up, he was hoping to be able to afford a car after the war.

The group returned late that night, and I could hear the laughter and happy voices when the car pulled up. I waited impatiently for my mother to come up the elevator. She looked tired and weary, but not happy. "Did you find a place?" I asked.

"Yes, but — well, it's a place — you know, everyone liked it and they all took something — so, what could I do? — I took something too."

"What's wrong? Why aren't you happy?"

She quickly explained it was not her choice. It was a farm house with a communal kitchen and dining room. Everyone would share stoves, tables, and the refrigerator. She had chosen a room with our own bath and shower. No lake, no river, no pool. "I just hope you are not disappointed Rosalind."

I was stunned, — a communal kitchen! My mother hated that. If she had been able to go alone with my father she would have dismissed, out of hand, any such idea. Women who shared those kitchen arrangements were the constant butt of Catskill jokes by stand-up comedians. There were legendary stories about hair-pulling "cat-fights" among women protecting their pots and pans, spoons and forks, refrigerator spots.

All I could say was, "No swimming? How come?"

"They just didn't think it was important," she said. "Besides one of the families couldn't afford more and no one else wanted to shop around."

That was the crux. They all agreed so that no one would be left out. I knew she could have begged off, but her need to get away from the city outstripped every other consideration. "They're such nice people," she said. "I'm sure it will be fine."

As for me, I was upset, but not about the communal kitchen. That could be fun. There would be friendly people, and children to keep Robert company. But the absence of any swimming nearby was incomprehensible. The area was awash with lakes, streams, swimming holes, a river and some pools. Even in the city we had access to swimming. All we could plan to do this summer was shower. It was a depressing prospect, but I would not say anything to hurt my mother. It had been a tough enough choice for her to make. She didn't need me to second guess her now. Besides it was only early March and we had plenty of time to think about it before July.

Instead, I sat down and wrote Chick a letter bemoaning my fate. It served to alleviate my frustration and disappointment. Three and a half weeks later, when I received his response, I had resolved most of my feelings about the summer choice. Mountains, trees, fields of grass, winding lanes and farms, gentle mornings and cool evenings, star-lit skies — it would be a good way to spend July and August. I loved the country. I could do without the frills.

But, when Chick's reply arrived, instead of words of sympathy and understanding, I received an explicit list of sensible things I should have done, along with comments that implied my father, in particular, should have done more. How did my father get into this? The letter enraged me. I quickly responded in anger telling him he could make decisions about his army life but that he didn't know diddle about my life. All I needed from him was a bit of sympathy. His suggestions were less than helpful and his inferences about my folks intolerable.

Another three and one half weeks later the following poem arrived.

❖

April 45
Burma

Dearest Darling Ros,

Why should I get excited and start tearing you apart, when I know that the anger you displayed did not come from your heart?

Can you help it if you read my letter and misinterpreted its meaning, and to let off steam you sat right down, to give me an awful beaning?

I said, "Maybe you ought to save your dough, rather than spend it at this time" even if it didn't please you, was it such a crime?

Then I said, "If go you must, why not to a pleasant spot", and then "for three or four weeks, yours would be a happy lot."

Did I say that "Your dad is wealthy and he should pay your way?

Did I even infer that he meet the bills for your stay?

See now, my dear I only meant that if you were to go
at all, then the thing I suggested was that you get on the
ball.

Why pay for a place, where you wouldn't have much
fun, why to a spot where swimming there is none.

Get angry if you must, after all, that's your right but
don't you think you were really out-of-sight?

I give you cause for anger true, yet this was not the case
So where do you get off to toss a brickbat in my face?

❖

Chick's choice of poetry was wise. I laughed out loud when I read
it. Yes, he meant no harm, he was just too far away. One thing became
clear to me then. Self pity is an indulgence. It does not warrant
sympathy. There is just one real solution — get on with your life —
exactly what I had been doing.

It was now the end of April, and I had put the whole incident
behind me. The "letter life" had strung our conversation out over two
months, but while we wrote and argued about the summer yet to come,
other things were happening during the March and April weeks.

The weather had improved rapidly. March had breezed in with
delightfully warm days, yet I treated each day as a gift, fully expecting
a freeze to blow in one more time. In April the high school would be
open evenings for adult activities. It was the spring semester — a
wonderful time to get out for some recreation.

Talking it over with some friends, three of us decided to take two
evenings a week to use the gym facilities and pool. We then discovered that, though the school was an all girls' high school, this program
would be co-ed. We joked about the possibility of the "boys getting
fresh" and wondered briefly whether the two husbands, who would
be baby sitting at home, would object. We laughingly agreed we were
old enough to handle whatever might come up and too old for anyone

to bother us anyway. At twenty-two, I was the youngest, the others were twenty-five.

The evenings were just what I needed. We played Ping-Pong, took turns at the stationary bicycle, worked the calisthenics equipment, and when we'd had enough, we topped the evening off with a swim in the Olympic size pool. The men who attended came to enjoy the same things we did — a break from the working day, some physical exercise and friendly, social interaction.

I don't recall making any new friends at the gym. All I remember is that the evenings, together with Chick's poetry brought a smile to my eyes and a lift to my step through lonely April and May days. Here are the poems.

20 April 45, India

My Dearest Darling Rosalind,

What love is this? It lifts me high to heaven
Where every angel is you.
And the joy of thinking of you fills me
With bursting happiness and my heart
Beats fast and my very blood boils at
The mention of your name.

What love is this? When in the quiet
Of the nite, when all is still, my thoughts
Are filled with you. And thru closed eyelids
I see you before me, sweet, lovable, and
Adoring. Holding your hand, walking by
Your side. Together, always together, at work,
Play or dreaming.

What love is this? That fills me with
Longing and then with mad desire.
To crush you to my heart and press my
Lips to yours; to feel my heart pounding
In unison with yours; to feel the warmth
Of your body and hear you whisper words
That are of love, as we reach exalted heights.
This Love is you!

2 May 1945, India

Dearest Darling Rosalind,

Light of my love, oh sweetest one
Thoughts of you calm my troubled soul
And like caresses, soothe me and soon
I am contented and relaxed, whole
I love you, with the tender passion
Of a true heart, with the fullness
Of my being. I adore you my loved
One, my dearest, my own!

The New York Times
April 11, 1945
*Courtesy of The New York Times Co.*

The New York Times
May 1, 1945
*Courtesy of The New York Times Co.*

"All the News That's Fit to Print"

# The New York Times

VOL. XCIV..No. 31,861.    NEW YORK, TUESDAY, MAY 1, 1945    THREE CENTS

# THE WAR IN EUROPE IS ENDED!
# SURRENDER IS UNCONDITIONAL;
# V-E WILL BE PROCLAIMED TODAY;
# OUR TROOPS ON OKINAWA GAIN

## ISLAND-WIDE DRIVE

**Marines Reach Village a Mile From Naha and Army Lines Advance**

**7 MORE SHIPS SUNK**

**Search Planes Again Hit Japan's Life Line— Kyushu Bombed**

By WARREN MOSCOW

GUAM, Tuesday, May 1—

### Leopold Rescued By 7th Army Troops

## The Pulitzer Awards For 1944 Announced

## MOLOTOFF HAILS BASIC 'UNANIMITY'

He Stresses Five Points as One Is Questioned

By JAMES B. RESTON

SAN FRANCISCO, May 1—

### PRAGUE SAYS FOES ACCEPT SURRENDER

Czechoslovak Radio Reports All Fighting in Bohemia Will Be Ended Today

LONDON, Tuesday, May 1—

GERMANY SURRENDERS: NEW YORKERS MASSED UNDER SYMBOL OF LIBERTY

*Thousands filling Times Square in spontaneous celebration yesterday*

### Wild Crowds Greet News In City While Others Pray

By FRANK S. ADAMS

### SHAEF BAN ON AP LIFTED IN 6 HOURS

Action Comes After Protests From Newspapers and Public
—Writer Still Barred

## GERMANS CAPITULATE ON ALL FRONTS

### American, Russian and French Generals Accept Surrender in Eisenhower Headquarters, a Reims School

### REICH CHIEF OF STAFF ASKS FOR MERCY

Doenitz Orders All Military Forces of Germany To Drop Arms—Troops in Norway Give Up —Churchill and Truman on Radio Today

By EDWARD KENNEDY

REIMS, France, May 7—Germany surrendered unconditionally to the Western Allies and the Soviet Union at 2:41 A. M. French time today. [This was at 8:41 P. M. Eastern Wartime Sunday.]

The surrender took place at a little red schoolhouse that is the headquarters of Gen. Dwight D. Eisenhower.

The surrender, which brought the war in Europe to a formal end after five years, eight months and six days of bloodshed and destruction, was signed for Germany by Col. Gen. Gustav Jodl. General Jodl is the new Chief of Staff of the German Army.

The surrender was signed for the Supreme Allied Command by Lieut. Gen. Walter Bedell Smith, Chief of Staff for General Eisenhower.

It was also signed by Gen. Ivan Susloparoff for the Soviet Union and by Gen. Francois Sevez for France.

[The official Allied announcement will be made at 9 o'clock Tuesday morning when President Truman will broadcast a statement and Prime Minister Churchill will issue a V-E Day proclamation. Gen. Charles de Gaulle also will address the French at the same time.]

General Eisenhower was not present at the signing, but immediately afterward General Jodl and his fellow delegate, Gen. Admiral Hans Georg Friedeburg, were received by the Supreme Commander.

**Germans Say They Understand Terms**

They were asked sternly if they understood the surrender terms imposed upon Germany and if they would be carried out by Germany.

They answered Yes.

Germany, which began the war with a ruthless attack upon Poland, followed by successive aggressions and brutality in internment camps, surrendered with an appeal to the victors for mercy toward the German people and armed forces.

After having signed the full surrender, General Jodl said he wanted to speak and received leave to do so.

"With this signature," he said in soft-spoken German, "the German people and armed forces are for better or worse delivered into the victors' hands."

## Summary of News of the War and German Surrender

TUESDAY, MAY 1, 1945

Chapter 14

# A TIME TO MOURN — A TIME TO REJOICE    1945

The European war was winding down; the days seemed to fly away. At the end of March the Russians moved on Berlin as the Allies crossed the Rhine.

On April 12, President Roosevelt died. When the news came over the radio, my mother and I stood frozen in place. We could not speak. There had been rumors that he was not well, but we attributed such comments to gossip mongering by the opposition press. When she could speak, my mother's first words were, "I knew he shouldn't have gone out in that open car that cold rainy day."

We cried along with millions of others in the country for a man who had been a great leader and inspiration, not only to us in the U.S., but also, to millions more around the world. He had mobilized us from being miserably unprepared to fight to "an arsenal of democracy," a nation of unmatched military might. We had produced enough war materiel to supply all our allies, and fight both the European and Asian wars. We cried also because he, of all people, would not see the war end, and it was now so close to the end. And we cried because we did not know Truman yet, and did not see him as a strong leader. I would miss Eleanor Roosevelt as well. I admired her. With her in the White House to remind the President, I knew that along with soldiers, the working families, men, women, and our children would not be forgotten because of the war.

In the last week of April the two Russian armies linked up inside Berlin giving them control over one fourth of the city. Truman, Churchill, and Stalin had agreed they would accept only an unconditional surrender and on April 30th, Hitler and Eva Braun committed suicide. On May 7, The European war was over.

Only a few weeks earlier, the streets had been filled with grieving people, mourning the death of their president. Now, wild crowds danced in the streets as radios broadcast the ecstatic shouts and blasting horns of celebrations. Movie houses everywhere showed films of thousands in jubilant revelry. I shivered with the excitement that heralded the end of the Hitler horror. But mine was a muted celebration. A few friends and I shared drinks and toasted the wonderful news.

I remained glued to the radio. Chick would not be coming home until the war in Asia was won. Rumors circulated that men would be shipped directly from the European theater to the Pacific. They were the kind of experienced soldiers needed to fight the Japanese. It was a sobering thought.

So many lives had been lost, but no one was thinking of that just now. Under the surrender headlines in the *New York Times*, you could read the news of the Asian war — a vivid reminder that men were still fighting a formidable war, one in which the enemy continued to claim that they would fight to the last man.

The speed of the armies crossing the Continent, the battles won, the march to victory these past months gave wings to the days. For a little while, time seemed to move faster.

Watching Robert helped speed my days. I marveled at the way he could conceptualize. One week he would enjoy having a story read to him, the following week he would understand that the letters formed words that told the story. Within days he would turn each page reciting the tale as though he were reading it to me; his vocabulary expanded daily. The inevitable "Why?" followed everything I said. Every day, he would surprise us with new ways of using his toys. Building blocks became a bridge, a train, a house, a road, or imaginary things. He needed more and more difficult puzzles to ponder. He loved dumping ten of them all over the floor at one time, always able to find the right piece for each puzzle. His dexterity with crayons and pencils was improving as well. Just a few short months had passed, but his learning came in giant leaps. I was discovering, like parents before me, that children learn more in their first two and one half years than we can ever imagine.

I hated that Chick was missing these new exciting developments. All I could do was write him, as best I could, filling in the missing moments with detailed stories and photos. Though film was rationed, we could always get some, which we used sparingly.

Chick continued to write as well. In his letter on May 8, he makes reference to the end of the war, then loses himself in poetry once again. I saved only the first page.

❖

8 May 1945
India

Dearest Sweetest Wife,
Tonite, when part of the world at least is living with peace, and this part of the world has succumbed to shadow, and only the stars and a part of the moon are out to challenge the stygian darkness, I am once again with you.

Have you sat on a lonely cliff, with only
The sound of lapping waves to remind
You that there are other lands, across the sea?

Have you strolled a winding lane,
Hidden from the sky by overhanging boughs
And heard only the crickets saying, "You are not alone?"

Have you lied down to dream,
And being unable to snare Morpheus,
Toss restlessly, thru the nite, until I came to you?

He is not alone, who loves as I do!
For always, no matter the worlds that
Separate us, you are with me.

Beside me, hearing the seas sing out
Of wonders that lie beyond the horizon
You are with me,
tho you are the wonder of whom they tell

Side by side, hand in hand, we stroll
Down the winding lane and the crickets sing
Of beauty. All their songs are of you.

Once more we are together, and next to my side
You recline, with your warm body pressed close
To mine, your blood running thru my veins

Now Morpheus comes to contented souls,
And I am content. For you are with me
Again, as always you will be in dreams.

❖

I believe Chick was moved to Chittagong, India, which put fewer miles between their base and the areas they were supplying in Burma. This short letter, with pictures of the town, and the cynical remarks of a tired soldier, is followed by more reveries with only the poem page saved.

❖

17 May 45
India

Dearest Darling Ros,

It's almost midnite right now, and for the last five minutes I wavered between writing and sleeping — and decided to make a stab at this. I was "on nites" again, and I had a fairly rough time of it — not bad, just busy. So much so that I didn't have time to write and that is most unusual. There was no mail tonite, and tho I thought that I'd at least get No. 150, still I don't feel badly about it. Tomorrow, I'll surely get some sweet letters from you.

Yesterday, I received a letter from Bill Falk, remember? He shipped overseas sometime in January and landed with an Air Depot Group in England. It's part of the Ninth Troop Carrier command. He's not doing classification work either; just working as a clerk typist at headquarters there. He's not happy with the job, but then he says he doesn't work hard at all. He was getting set to go to London on a three-day pass, so I suppose that like Larry — he's got it made.

I'm really feeling swell these days, altho terribly tired right now. The weather is hot, but hell, it can't get me down when the sweat rolls down, I take a shower and that's that. If it's very hot at nite, I toss and roll and then fall asleep. Let the days come, and spend themselves and move on. Like the river, I go on' and if I keep going long enough.. I'll get to you! And that's all I hope for, pray for, and live for.

I got your film quickly but I haven't taken any pictures as yet. But tho I don't have any of me to send, I've got others that I'll enclose tonite. I'll give you some idea of what the pictures portray and hope that will make up in some small way, the brevity of this letter.

No. 1. Street Scene, The place looks a hell of a lot better here than thru a person's eyes. Here the impression is that the street is wide. — Don't believe it. — What makes this look, really good, is the fact that you can't smell the "smells."

No. 2. This scene is laid where girls are "layed." This area in town is known as "Jig-Jig Lane," a neighborhood that abounds with whores and is "off limits." Notice the bamboo walls of their huts.

*1. One of the main streets in town - India*

*2. The court between buildings. This place is Jig-Jig Lane*

No. 3. Who this one is, I don't know (need I add that?). She is probably one of those "Jig-Jig" girls. She is seated and really in the process of eating. Indians squat this way always. They almost never sit on chairs, boxes etc. All the eating utensils they use, is their five fingers, assuming they use only one hand.

No. 4. This is a pagoda, somewhere in Burma, right near where our planes landed at a "forward strip." The insides are stuccoed with bright stones and glass.

No. 5. No travelogue of India is sufficient without something like this. If you look closely you can count some different kinds of snakes. They seem quite subdued however. Maybe they're hungry like the rest of the Indians.

God, they look nothing like Artie Shaw!

*3. A Local Belle*

*4. Burmese Pagoda*

*5. India, Snake Charmer*

No. 6. This looks better than it is, which is the case in almost all of these photos. Some kind of Mohammedan Temple. Maybe then again, it's Hindu!

No. 7. Who built this or how is unknown to me. Probably the only building in town which would remain standing if a fire swept the town. Probably built by the British back in 1880, as an outpost for the famed Bengal Lancers.

That's all of them for now. I'll try to get some shots of "Rangoon" from this fellow and send them along soon.

Tonite, I'll probably fall dead asleep the moment my head hits the sack. If no dreams come, then I'll be angry as hell for having to work so hard and getting so tired.

I love you, my darling. So very, very much, so very deeply.

Days keep going by and I speed them onward. Closer and closer, we come to that wonderful day of our reunion.

You are all my life

I love you alone.

Always and Forever,
CHICK

Yes, you are all that my hopes have aspired to. You are all my dreams come true. Here as I sit, almost in semi-darkness because lights have still not been installed, I lean back now and then and try to recapture some episode of years back. And since our lamps (kerosene) are giving us much

*6. House of Worship - India*

*7. Used now as a British Hospital*

157

more trouble than is usual I lean back now and then to rest my eyes. As I did so this last time, I started putting more words together. Can you make any sense of this:

"ODE TO A FLICKERING LAMP
OR IT'S ABOUT TIME THEY INSTALLED THE ELEC-
TRIC LIGHTS SO I CAN WRITE MY BABY, WHILE
SWEATING IT OUT IN THE CBI"

The lamplight flickers and fades
Darkness hastens to cover all
That but a short moment ago
Was light. The shadows fall!

In the lonely quiet of this cool night
No sounds are heard, no living thing
Is here, to trouble my reverie
As my heart listens, to my memory sing.

Its songs are of beauty and of you
For both are one, even as you and I
They weave a pattern, frail as lace
The story of love that will never die

Love that sparkles, bright and gay,
That welcomes joy and banishes tears,
That warms the heart and bids laughter stay
To aid in conquering all our fears.

The songs are old, but love is new
These moments divine are such a treasure
For a little while, as the shadows fell,
They brought me darkness, and so much pleasure.

I keep hoping that the mail men are not screwing up and that I'll get some mail tomorrow. I haven't heard from you in several days now. But that's just the price we pay when we get a batch and get them quickly. We always have to sweat out the .....

*India 1945*

*India 1945*
*Chick with 3 friends*

Chapter 15

# MENTAL JOUSTS, SEX HYGIENE AND LOSS 1945

Now that the European war was ended, all of the country's strength and energy was concentrated on the Asian War. The Japanese had pushed into every corner of the Pacific ocean. We had fighting units in places we never knew existed, places with strange sounding names — Bataan, Iwo Jima, Okinawa, New Guinea, Guam, Wake Island, The Mariana and Marshall Islands, Biak, Leyte, and New Caledonia.

Despite the importance of the area where Chick was stationed, the China Burma Indian Theater (CBI) received scant coverage in the news. How troops were supplied was not headline news in 1945, nor did we receive detailed information on deaths and wounded in the way we do today with TV coverage. As a result I have learned most of the facts that follow from my research of the combat cargo squadrons.

In 1942, the Japanese had overrun Rangoon and moved up the Irrawaddy River through Mandalay and Myitkyina, cutting off the Burma Road and all access to China. Burma was therefore placed under total Japanese domination. Nothing could be done to win back the countries and Islands unless an effective way could be found to supply the fighting units. All roads were either cut off or non existent. Supply ships were sunk regularly by Japanese submarines. Air supply was the only answer, and the Combat Cargo Groups were organized to do the job.

When Chick arrived in December 1944, progress had already been made. Myitkyina had been liberated and the British were pushing the Japanese back and out. As the battle fronts moved further south, the distances the cargo planes needed to fly in order to deliver supplies became longer and longer. This meant that Chick was further and further away from where the action was.

The tonnage carried and the mileage covered for one month alone was staggering. The total tonnage hauled was 26,055 tons; the mileage flown was estimated to be almost 3,000,000 miles for the April, 1945 operations into Burma.

The Japanese defeat was nearly complete. Their forces split, they were cut off from all means of escape. As the British-Indian units advanced, the Combat Cargo Task Forces, using C-46s, participated in a final surprise move. On May 2 they dropped hundreds of paratroopers south of Rangoon[1] to finish the drive.

By the end of May few missions were being flown. Chick, along with others, were facing more and more hours and days with little of interest to keep them busy.

How did the men keep going when they were back on base? What did they do?

From their first days in India, each time the pilots and crews returned from a mission they were entitled to two shots of liquor. At first everyone lined up quickly for his drinks. Within a week or two, most men became impatient with the line-up. The lines were too long and they were too tired. It just wasn't worth it. The liquor piled up, and before long, combat cargo group clubs were set up instead.

I'm sorry I did not keep the letters from Chick describing how he helped set up the club in their section. It reminded him of our Lewisohn Stadium days. But instead of selling beer and soda, the drinks here were free. In time, I believe the club carried soda and snacks as well. It was a gathering place where the men could meet, play cards, recount the events of the day, gripe, discuss or just unwind. For a while, Chick enjoyed working the bar and organized the stock. When there was time, he would schmooze with a few friends.

As May drew to a close, he began to spend less and less time at the club, and more and more time writing to me. I was rewarded with many wonderful letters and poems during this period. Here are a few.

❖

1    from *It Began at Imphal: The combat Cargo* Story by John G. Martin, D.V.M. 1988 Sunflower University Press.

22 May 45
India

My Dearest Darling,

The days seem to be gathering momentum as they pass. Somehow they pass so quickly for me that I don't seem to recall some of them. I guess that the first six months are the hardest. These days I just drift along, maintaining a pretty even temperament. I don't give a good God damn about anything — don't care if I work or not, don't care if school keeps or not. When I do feel like doing something, I go to it with a will, and what I don't care to do, I don't. And surprisingly enough, for quite a while, I've been feeling just that way and feeling damn good.

I sit around quite a bit and apparently I'm not doing a damned thing. But actually the old brain is rolling along. I have mental jousts with myself. On various occasions I have reviewed my theory concerning "Labor Relations — A Human Approach," or The Peace Conference and its chances of success; me and you and the rest of the world, etc. I think about various things, some serious like the above and some rather comical, and I feel a mental exhilaration as a result of it.

I'm learning more and more to live with myself. And tho I never thought that I'd be good company for myself, I find now that I can bear it, and what's more, get a kick out of it now and then. Yes, every now and then during the course of a day, I still get involved in discussions with others, but more often than not, they're quite inane. And more often than not, it's my own fault.

Mostly, I get wound up and in twenty minutes I try to explain things it took me so many years of formal education to learn, and years of experience to prove or disprove. And so, speaking volubly and forcefully, I rush on, and my thoughts come cascading forth, I lose them on the first turn, and soon I'm aware that I'm talking way over my head. So I stop and regret that I ever started.

Trouble is that I should listen more — But then I never was a good listener. Yet I'm learning how and recently I've been keeping fairly quiet and so I annoy myself least in that way. But when I do get together with myself — I really let loose and I think all the thoughts that I might have expressed, but didn't. So far it's working out fairly well. More and more, I'm learning to come in and read or write or drink without working behind the bar or feeling that I own the place, and so attend to everything personally. There too I'm striking a happy balance.

I have been spending quite a lot of time in the office this past week, and last nite, after writing you, I thought it would be nice to get to town for a look-see. I mentioned it casually to the officer and he approved. So off to town I went and what I thought would be a quick visit turned out to be a damn nice frolic.

It's difficult to explain — I felt free as I hit town. I strolled leisurely, not caring to "get" to any particular place. And so I was able to be more observing and more peaceful too. I was less intolerant of the masses of humanity that the crooked streets spewed forth. Of late, I found myself becoming bitter at their shortcomings and filth and their "cattle-like" approach to life. Now today, as I mingled with them, they were alive, intensely so; and their squalor, tho still there, was relegated to the background. I saw them only as little people hurrying to their appointed tasks. And I wondered, and then decided that formerly my approach was "too American." Everything about this country I would compare with things back home. And these people suffered so by comparison. As I wandered thru town my attitude softened greatly and I must then have decided to try to meet an Indian who would reaffirm for me my faith in humanity. But first I must have lunch. So I trundled up to the RAF Club. I must say that I had a better lunch than I would have gotten on the base. First, liver and onions and chips (french fried potatoes) and then pancake with sugar and lime, and to wash it down, a glass of lime water. It doesn't sound like much, but I was eminently pleased with it. I sat in the lounge and discovered a Calcutta paper, three days old and devoured it eagerly. But I couldn't stay much longer, I had to get along on my quest!

As I left the club, I noticed a "Garry" nearby. This is a very flimsy carriage, drawn by two runt sized horses. I strode up and said: "My man, a spin around town, if you please." I was regarded with a blank stare and plaintively he answered, "Sahib?" I bounced in, yelled "Let's go" — He smiled, climbed on and we took off. Spurring his horses to their utmost, we made, after nearly exhausting them, top speed of 3 to 5 miles an hour. After an hour of sightseeing, at one part of town I came to a sign — "M. Dasistra, Pleader, _____Court!" Here's my man," I shouted and in due time I made it clear to the driver that this was the end of the line. I rewarded him liberally with a lot of smiles but few, too few rupees and sauntered over to the "office" of this kindred spirit. With a "Good day, do you mind if I come in?" I proceeded to make myself comfortable and he was friendly as all hell.

He was taller than I, with a good looking face, clean, bare to the waist with a long cotton sheet wound intricately around the lower part of his body. Tall as he was, he must have weighed 60 lbs less than I did. I explained quickly that all I wanted to do was to talk with him and that I hoped he was not too busy to do so. After his assurance that he wasn't (see, just like home!), I explained that I studied law in America, and it being my lot to come to India I wanted to get a better idea of what made this country tick. And my speaking acquaintanceship with names like Gandhi, Nehru, Muslim League, Mrs. Pandit, (who incidentally is Indian's unofficial delegate to the San Francisco Peace Conference) and Tagore, was like an open sesame.

Soon we were really enjoying a pleasant chat. In the course of it, I listened mostly while in fairly good English he painted a picture of India, its customs, mores, hopes and longings. Not calculated to arouse my sympathy, it did none-the-less, and I could think back and visualize other men, at other times, talking of freedom, liberty and opportunity as tho these were "dream words." Here, 175 years later, was a man who spoke as Tom Paine and Jefferson did. And I couldn't help but realize that some day their voices would be heard in the House of Parliament.

Here was renewed hope and faith for India. He spoke of the caste system as a "shackle" along with British Imperialism. He cursed the famines that visit his people periodically. He thanked America for her generosity and welcomed the thought that American capital might be invested in this country. He had a profound knowledge of world events, fully cognizant of the mighty role we play and aware of Russia's new influence. I found as we went along that he was interesting and well informed. A credit to any country and any civilization.

Of necessity, our talk came to an end, after two hours flew by, and we parted, with me promising to visit him again, if I could, and him expressing his heartfelt thanks at my unexpected and pleasant visit.

I left feeling refreshed and passed several shops on my way to the main road. Just to prove how good I felt, I wanted to buy something, to send you, your mother and mine, so that you might all share my mood - even if in so circumvented a manner.

So I bought some knickknacks for the house made of bell metal. They are attractive little dishes, with hand painted designs. They are probably useless, but they look quite good and very possibly they may serve as a receptacle for jam, sugar, candy, etc. I also included a receptacle, which stands on a tricky wooden affair. This is meant to house flowers and serve as a centerpiece. Since I envisage fresh flowers in our home often, save this for us. There are six small dishes and these you should divide between our mothers.

In addition, I'm sending along those "leather unstuffed cushions," which were bought more than a month ago, intended as a mother's day gift. Again, one for each of the two!

I speak as tho I've sent them already. I have not. But I did get the box, the paper, the string etc. Tomorrow, come hell or high water, off it goes. Since it will travel via boat, you will have to wait months for it, but when it comes, you'll think back and recall this day. A pretty damn good one for me.

After buying these things, I hopped a ride back to camp and arrived in time for a roast chicken dinner. Lucky? You bet!

Then a visit to the day room, and a couple of cokes and some pleasant banter with some GI's around.

Then a comfortable seat at a table, my pen, paper and you. The clock has pointed its hands to ten, and my eyes tell me it's bed time. Yes, another day is past, forgetting to bring with it its usual quota of boredom, monotony and despair.

I suppose if I were to delve for a reason for all this, I could attribute it to the letter I got last nite and the one I wrote in return. I glowed as I read it and answered it, and it was as tho fresh blood was being pumped thru my body. This morning too, I awoke happy and I head for bed this way.

There was no mail tonite but I expect some tomorrow and maybe there'll be some more tenderly loving letters from you. These will be reactions to that series I sent you early in May, with those shots of me.

I love you my darling, so fully, so passionately. My life is you and my love you have always been. My hope tonite, is that there are days that are not too hard for you to take. But one day, this will end and we'll be together again.

> Dearest Darling Rosalind,
> I love only you,
> CHICK

23 May 1945
India

Dearest Darling Rosalind;

Is it odd that when a cool zephyr breeze
Gently washes the steaming heat away
That I think of you, and the touch of your hand?

Strange, is it? That birds in the trees
Should sing of my love, who every day
Is near me, not in a far away land?

How else can it be? Your heart entwined in mine
Will always remain. And they beat as one
Thru endless Day and lonely Night.

When my step is quick it's but a sign
That my thoughts are of you. And when day is done
Often I smile, for you come into sight

I love you. Tenderly, as raindrops falling on a rose.
I love you. Sincerely, as one makes a vow.
I love you. Passionately, as the blazing sun.

You are my life. Of all the world's wonders, I chose
For my wife, the one I write to now
Whose body and soul, and mine too, are one.

This day was a contrast to yesterday in every respect
other than the fact that today I still feel pretty damn good.

Today, I hung around the office all day, reading a little, working a little, just doing nothing a little, and that coupled with eating and showering disposed of most of it. There was no mail, and so at 5:30 I came back to the office, where I was "on duty" again tonite. Now at 9:30 I have only a bit more to do, before fulfilling my army obligations. Just another very pleasant day overseas!

After a spell of fairly nice weather, at about 6:30, the skies muttered threats, which soon turned into a driving rainstorm. As tho to help, Aeolus unleashed his winds, but our tent (office) withstood the onslaught, the floor becoming our only casualty. But a broom helped out and we were very comfortable. As a result, the air now is so much cooler and fresher. What seemed at first to be destructive, proved to be beneficial. Right now, the rain is done, but this area abounds with many small sized lakes. Several days of this and we'll be swimming from place to place. It's a trifle early for the monsoons, so I suppose we'll have some really nice days left.

My boss came back today after spending five days in Calcutta, and now after doing only two things in the morning tomorrow, I'm to have the rest of the day off. That should be spent in fishing all of my clothes out of the bottom of my barracks bag and airing them out. They haven't seen the light of day for six months. I wonder how moldy they are?

But I'll probably not even do that. I'll be found doing one of these two things instead. 1) Just sitting around, sun bathing, sleeping.

2) Going to town, maybe to look up my friend. Are there any other possible alternatives?

There was one constructive thing that I did. I got the package all wrapped and mailed. There is a possibility that it may get to you quickly. On that chance, I sent it first class and paid the equivalent of $4.20 to Uncle Sam. Nick sent a package like that a month ago and it was received in 9 days. It weighed just about the same, almost nine pounds. I hope that our mothers and you can find some use for them! As a result of all this, my finances are pretty badly mauled, but solvent condition. See how I've learned?

Incidentally, I sent you another package about 3 days ago, ordinary mail, which consisted of 2 cartons of cigarettes and 2 cartons of Wrigley's chewing gum. Ordinarily, I suppose, that shouldn't be done, but I had them and didn't need them, (for now we all have more than enough) so I sent them to you and you and Robert can put them to good use. I also enclosed a carton of Raleighs. I don't recall now in which package you'll find it, but when you do, give them to your mom. As I recall, "thems her Brand."

You must have noticed by now that I use two sides of the paper now. The reasons are that (1) there is a temporary shortage of thin sheets here at the office, (2) nothing I write anymore can be construed to convey any military information, so there is no fear of the censor cutting things out, which would result in mutilating innocent passages on the reverse side.

Tonite, it's only a bit difficult to get going because I hoped for mail but none came. These next letters from you should be very interesting. Have you decided on what you can do toward getting some special shots of you? Or have you had them taken already?

I have re-read the last two letters time and time again. They were exceptionally long and fine too. One thing about them is the fact that the latest one #155 has your admission that "your cycle" theory, is not entirely a valid one. In your previous letter, you were so convinced that it was. Menstruation is definitely a release for you, but how easily you can be aroused when a tender letter from me comes, when the "heat" is off. For me, your letters have just about the same effect no matter when they come. What to do about it then, when I'm restless and jumpy and can think only of you. Those pictures of you should be a great help. I can lie in bed and with the aid of a flash light, see you before and beside me.

If you react to all the letters I sent last month, in the same manner as you did when you read my letters of 30 April and 1 May, then you'll have a pretty rough month. And I in turn, will have a good one too, from the end of this month to the middle of next.

One of the fellows here had one of those little books that are to be found everywhere soldiers are. The story of "Erotic Edna," who seems to have been quite a whore. While he hung around the office, he asked me if I would like to read it. I glanced at it and skimmed thru a few pages. Quite a book, it must be. I don't know, for I put it down after a few minutes. It didn't excite me half as much or one quarter as much as your letters can. I don't know why I didn't read it thru. Wasn't in the mood I guess. I just didn't care.

Do women go for stories like these, or have any of the girls ever shown you "poems" etc. I wonder, have you ever read one of them; would you like to?

They are easily obtainable here, and should I read one and think it interesting would you want me to send it?

The days keep going as you see, and they are piling up. I haven't heard the news lately but I guess our planes fly over Tokyo fairly often. More and more these visits will increase and they'll be ready for the kill.

God, how I pray that it be soon. I ache to be with you again, and with Robert living the wonderful life that will be ours.

You are all I love,
until eternity, you alone.
CHICK

❖

During his flight overseas, Chick commented on the rampant venereal disease in Africa. It was not a matter of concern for either of us. We wrote freely about personal things; sex and the army were amusing subjects, and porno books circulated all over the base. I answered each of Chick's queries, — did I ever see one? "No;" — would I like to? "I don't need that;" — an interesting one? "Sure!" I never received a book, but the following sheets arrived. I laughed out loud when I read them as did every friend who saw them.

Headquarters were trying very hard to educate the men, but they didn't seem to have a sense of humor — or did they?

HEADQUARTERS
4TH COMBAT CARGO GROUP
APO 218 Theater

19 June 1945.


SEX HYGIENE
(Plain Talk)

I. FOR WISE ACRES: We know that you are going to "get as much of it as you can" until the day you die. That's your business.

    2. But, this is the Army's business:-

        a. That you use a condom and take a pro carefully, .

        b. That you report all sores of the private areas of the body at once because:

            (1) If you report it LOD (Line of duty)-Yes.

            (2) If someone else find it on you, LOD-No.

            (3) If you never report it, you willcripple yourself for life.

        c. That you cannot return to the stateswith V.D. You must complete treatment first.In the case of syphilis this takes 26 weeks.

        d. That you do nothing that will interfere with your job in the Army V.D., drinking on duty, etc.

174

e. To remind you that without good health, you and America have no future.

II. <u>FOR THOSE ON THE FENCE:</u>  1. We know that the boasts of the Wise Acres, the long separation from even a look at American girls, the longing for satisfaction of our natural desires, all add up to great temptations.

2. But remember:

a. The wise acres pays with disease, loss of self respect, unhappy married life, and even sterility (inability to get children).

b. If you stay clean, you will be able to return home with your head high and be able to look your sister, your mother, your wife, or your daughter in the eye and tackle the future with a clean slate.

c. You will be able to bring up your children (not deformed by your V.D.) to be clean living people. And you will have to set the example The sins of the fathers are visited on the children."

III. <u>For the truly wise:</u> 1.   Thank Heaven that you are our greatest number. You don't want a medal for being true to yourself and to your loved ones, to YOUR America, you

don't need lectures to tell you that to keep
yourself clean in mind and body is to make
life a beautiful adventure rather than a
dirty gutter. God Bless you for you are near-
est to Him.

IV. TIPS FROM THE "DOC:"   1. If you
really want to prevent V.D.-

> a. Wear a condom - this protects a
> small part of you.
>
> b. Take a pro. - this protects a
> little larger part of you.
>
> c. But take a complete hot, soapy
> bath - not one hour after - at once
> after intercourse. Only this will
> protect your whole body.
>
> d. In the CBI Theater; there are
> diseases which enter your skin
> (without a cut) along your legs,
> your belly, your lips. A condom and
> a pro are not enough.We have no
> treatment for some. The following
> diseases are prevalent in this theate:

| | | |
|---|---|---|
| Syphilis | Lymphogranuloma Inquinale | Crabs |
| Yaws | Granuloma Inquinale | 7 year itc |
| Fungus | Tropical Ulcer | Dhobie It |
| Leprosy | Gonorrhea | Chancroid |

> e. If all this is too much trouble,
> don't expose yourself.

   2. The treatment:

a. Gonorrhea (Clap) - with sulfa drug-75% effective with penicillin-90% effective

b. Syphilis: with arsenicals and bisumth-80% effective (blood text)

c. India V.D.: We have no specific treatment.

d. Leprosy: Tough Luck.

e. No treatment is 100% effective, or perfect.

3. If you are the incurable one - then your life is shot - suffering, deformed children, and early death.

V. **LAST NOTE:** The human body or mind does not suffer or dry up or get smaller or die early if you stay away from intercourse all your life.

A. J. MADONIA,
Captain, Medical Corps,

C _____ V.D. Officer

As time passed Chick grew more and more reflective. The letters said less but the poems kept coming. MY ODYSSEY was a recap of our lives, starting with the first date, the prom, throughout the years. It even explained LOVE IS GONE.

❖

"MY ODYSSEY, OR
HOW'S THESE FOR MEMORIES, BABY,
WHILE SWEATING IT OUT IN THE  CBI"

Years past, when much of life
Was new to me, and thoughts of taking a wife
Had not yet occurred, there were some girls
Who could on occasion put me in a whirl
By wearing a pretty frock, or by dancing
To the beat of the music, or by romancing
When stars were bright
And the pale moonlight
Got in my eyes.
    That was years ago, Not Now!

Then came the day, a million memories ago
I first saw you, and my heart warmed to a glow
At the sight of one, so young, beautiful, with such grace
And with the second glance at your well formed face
I had all I could to keep my heart from thumping
Yet it did. And my pulse started jumping.
The beauty that was you dazzled my eyes,
More than the brightest star in the skies.
    That was years ago, and it happens still.

You were Lovely, not like those who "practice" charm,
And I knew that it could never cause harm
To let myself go whither my heart would lead,
For tho, then, no thoughts came that I would need
You to live (as I know now I do) I thought
Such pleasures of knowing you could not be bought,
And she is young and I am too
Let's play the game of Love, the whole way thru
And we did!
                That was years ago, and we are at it still.


You were sweet and lovely, with an agile mind,
So alluring, (is that the right word?)
With countenance kind;
When after months of seeing you now and then,
Of dropping in to visit, when
My studies were done. To take a walk
Around the reservoir seemed right, and to talk
With you about this and that, and at the end
Of the evening my homeward way I'd wend,
With the taste of doughnuts and tea and Indian nuts
Still on my lips, instead of kisses. There were no "buts,"
But she's too young, But so am I,
But his work's not done, But she's not ready to try
To manage a household and then babies,"
There were only thoughts of sweet delight
As thinking of you, and at the sight
Of you, my heart would glow.
             That was years ago, and it glows still.

Then that first night, when all at once,
The heavens came down, and for the nonce
The cymbals clashed, the lightening flashed
And the sky crumbled like a teacup, dashed
To pieces on stone. A feeling of wonderful bliss,
Our first kiss!

Remember the night stars seemed to explode
And we two found ourselves on the road
To Love?
    That was years ago, we're on the road still.

Of sorrow, that night, there was not a trace
As the two of us stood, with the wind in our face
It was right, the world should end, and start anew
As life did for me and you.

And hours later, homeward bound at dawn,
A wonderful feeling burned that morn,
Brighter and hotter, to an all consuming flame
All because our hearts beat in the same
Tempo
    That was years ago. They are that way still.

  No more Dearest. If this attitude I have now doesn't escape me, I'll try to add some more tonite. I hope they get some lights in the Basha.
  I have to shower now and see if I can get to town.
  You are all I love, all my life. Maybe someday I can tell you of it.

Stay well and happy. My fondest hopes are with you. Take good care of yourself and Robert. Millions of kisses and caresses to both of you.

As Ever,

CHICK

❖

Many poems were written by army men during the war. Here is one. Unfortunately, we do not know the poet or poets since it is unsigned.

In the poem Assam is a reference to Sylhet and Agartala. Burma refers to Myitkyina.

## "THE TOUGHEST OF THEM ALL"

-by-

Ab the Scab (over USAAF Radio Station VU2ZV, Chabua)
As Modified and Adapted by A.G.B. & J.B.L., 4 Comeargroup S-2

---

Three friends were standing at a bar;
Each smoking a big, fat, black, cigar;
Each was trying "to tie one on"
Each aware that he'd soon be gone;
For each had decided to go to war,
To keep the jap from his own back door;
But each, by some odd quirk of chance,
Had joined up in a different branch.
The Marine straightened, on unsteady feet,
His face quite filled with great conceit;
"When the war is over, we'll meet again,
And I'll tell you some stories of real he-man!"
The sailor smiled our: "Brother, you will learn,
When you hear from me on my return."
The Soldier first said not a word,
Tossed off another, then averred:
"I'll neither boast nor brag, my men,
Until I'm sure I'm back again."
Where upon they made a farewell bet,
And on this plan their minds were met:
The one whose story was the best,
Should have the drinks on all the rest.

---

The war is over, and they are back,
Drinkin' 'em down in that same old shack.
The Marine, with ribbons spread o'er his chest,
Stands there in front of all the rest:
"I saw action in the far South Seas,
I dropped the nips from out the trees -
And wiped them out like hapless fleas;
Beat that my buddies, if you please!"
The Sailor gave a superior smile;
And, laughing at the Marine awhile,
Says: "Friends, I really saw the fight,
Off Italy, off France, and in the Reich,
I ferried John Doughboy across the Rhine,
And did some time on the firing line."
The Soldier listens without a word,
Looking amused and quite unperturbed.
Then he smacks the bar with resounding slam,     { SYLHET
Proudly boasts of his tour in fetid ASSAM,     — { . AGARTAL
And stoutly adds, in a boilermaker's murmur:
"What's more, by God, I sweated out BURMA!"
The Leatherneck gulps, and the Bluejacket too:     \ HJITKINA
"Jeez, Brother, we owe the drinks to you!"
For each had heard, and knows damn well,
That there stands a returnee straight from HELL.

Even in late May, though the flights were shorter and less frequent, and the enemy was mostly in retreat, there were still dangers

and losses. The one friend Chick mentioned frequently in his letters, Walter Formigly, was assigned a regular mission flight over the Hump ( a dangerous Himalayan mountain). His plane did not make it — he never returned.

I don't have the letter telling me what happened, but I do remember that Chick had described him as a decent, down-to-earth, intelligent man, a careful person, (pilot, I believe), who would not take unnecessary risks. They talked together about many things, and shared similar dreams. Walter's wife was pregnant and expecting their baby any day, a subject close to them both. Knowing Chick, I'm certain he found a place and a time to cry for this caring husband and father who died just as the Burma War was coming to an end.

It seemed to me that after Walter's death, the club held little interest for Chick. Conversations there didn't engage him any longer, they seemed pointless and foolish. He retreated more and more into himself and his dreams.

❖

## 29 May 45 India

Dearest Sweetest Rosalind;

Tonite, feeling as tho I'd like to chase the hours away, I went to the show here on the base. For a half an hour I sat and thought of you — for what better way to wait for "make believe" in the form of movies. I was miles from here — you and I alone were walking round the reservoir. — The nite, quite warm, with traces of the rain that fell earlier, took us to her bosom — At her call, the moon and stars, so brightly lighted our way. Alone, our hearts were singing our song of love as we started to make our dream.

I found us near the place where rolling waves come on shore and having kissed it, go back to the sea. And with each wave, to you, all my love I bare, and kissed you with each vow — These vows I made, I meant them all, and they will come true — someday, you'll see!

Once more, we too, were found so happy with our love, one sunny day in spring. We sat, and talked and tho I don't recall the very words — my heart does. It tells me now — that I kept saying —I love you darling dear, I do — I do. You smiled and held my hand in yours and pressed it to your cheek and tears peeped out — They peeped from under smiling eyes that held a promise true — of me — and you.

I saw again, the day that you and I were wed — The day that shall not die in memory. From that day on — we've lived our love and always will — That day we two were one. And then the years rolled slowly on to happiness and with them we came along.

Time passed as it will but left us with a little one, our son, who looks like us. Like us, he's love, he's life for us and joys are many now - He's ours to share.

We stand beside his bed and hold our hands as one — we smile and kiss. For love will live and grow even as our Robert does — so fine so true.

These dreams went on, until the clash of cymbals came to me, and shook me from my reverie!

Up until now I've been singing as I wrote these words. I just stopped and re-read them and noticed the curious phrasing, and seemingly disconnected thoughts. The song I've been humming and even singing these words aloud is "Goodnight sweet dreams, Sweetheart". That was one of the feature songs of the picture I saw — "Hollywood Canteen" Somehow, after I heard it first, I was hard put to it, to stop from singing it aloud each time the music subsequently appeared. And as I left the theater, I sang it while walking down the road. Enchanted by my dreams of you, I walked as tho I was alone in this part of the world. And as I sang, I was happy — for the words I sang were not found in the song — they were to be found only in my heart.

Remember how I'd do that occasionally. Mostly with little rhyme, and taking liberties with the music, I'd sing you a story. Tonite — for the first time since the States, I did that. Almost for the very first time too, I sang - or rather, my heart did. I love you so very much, Ros — I love you.

I can't recall too, having been so happy since last October, when we were on furlough. Really genuinely happy. What it is, I don't know, But all during these last few hours, it was just as tho you were by my side. The illusion was so perfect. I didn't see you — how could I — it was dark in the movies — and on the road. But I knew you were there - never questioned it for a moment. You didn't speak as we walked down the road, but then you never did, when I sang "these songs" for you.

Strange, how for a little while, the hardships and cares that weigh heavily upon me were forgotten. Somehow, you and your love got right to me, inside of me, to dispel them all. How grateful and thankful I am for that love. O my dearest sweetest Ros. I love you so.

Even now, I sing as I write these words and it's these words I sing. My love, my own, tomorrow will find me with you dear — you know, I know. Our love will last as long as love is known to anyone, as long as life. Thru all, the tears, the fears that may befall us, thru the years — one thing we'll have. Your smile, my song, your faith in me, my faith in you — our boy, our life, our love.

With that, alone, and nothing else, we'll see it thru, until one day, we'll be home. Our home, where we can live our love away, and with each passing day — we'll find that it shall grow more and more a lovely dream, the way we want it to be.

Yes dear — tonite— I think of all that's lovely, that is true. Tonite, it's only you.


Rosalind — I almost decided to end this letter here. It's just as tho I've been under a spell, woven by you, 10,000 miles away. But there are several things I wanted to write tonite even tho I had to sit here for fifteen minutes, to shake the spell, so I could write logically. There was no mail tonite, and I did so want to get the two letters — Nos.160-161, that the mail man owed me. Yet tomorrow they'll come, and tomorrow will be a better day, for their coming. It occurs to me, that with the use of air transport to carry men home, and also to this theater, that our mail service will suffer. Nothing official, it's just a thought, and I'm preparing myself for 14 and 16 day service. Maybe you ought to also, and if this fine service continues — we'll be pleasantly disappointed.

Then, I heard from a fellow here, who was a friend of Walter's that his wife spoke to Mr. Formigly too, and that Jo, as of the 14th (3 days after she was notified ) hadn't yet given birth. They say she couldn't sleep etc., and that they were very worried about her. What's happened since? Anything tough happen to her or the kid?

Another thing — as you noticed — I'm sending along this star sapphire. Held under the sunlight, you'll see an exceptionally bright star in the stone. Maybe you'll get the same effect under direct light from a lamp. It is much bigger than the average size around here and I paid much less for it. You'll notice a flaw in it, right around the center of the star. As a flaw, it's a very unusual one. I don't mind its existence there at all, in fact I think it adds something to the stone.

I like this, and hope that you do too. If you wish, put it into a setting or save it, along with the ruby. I don't expect to be able to get more stones very soon  maybe in a couple of weeks. I'd like to get a star ruby, this size or not much smaller. From time to time I may be able to get more. If I get enough  you'll be able to make up something more than just a ring. Maybe you'll be able to set them in a bracelet or make a pendant.

So far as a gift for Rebecca is concerned, I'll try to get something nice for them. They richly deserve it — And so do Bernie and Julia. I won't have too much money, but I'll try to get something. I'll send what I get to you and you can make distribution. Have you gotten this last package I sent as yet? I wanted it all to get to you quickly so I sent it first class. The postage cost about 1/5 of the entire cost. Maybe more!

I was hoping tonite, as I walked and sang that somehow I could make a recording of it and send it. For the first time in a long time, my voice sounded really good. Fellows who heard, looked up and were surprised to find it was me. You see I never did sing since coming over. As I write now, I can hear your voice, as it was on the record "Good-bye darling, I love you - so very much -please - love me too!"

Darling — my heart is yours, as all of me is. Nothing in the world is as certain or so unending as my love for you, and always with each passing day I love you more.

"Goodnight, sweet dreams / tomorrow is another day / Goodnight - sweet dreams / sweetheart".

I love only you.<br>
CHICK

I tried to call Jo. I think they lived in the mid-west, but when I couldn't connect with anyone, I didn't follow through. What could I say to her? It seemed to me my conversation could only bring her more pain. I think differently today. Knowing others are thinking of you and care, can bring comfort.

*Burma - 1945. At work.*

*Making friends in town*

*Sweeping up*

*The basha*

Chapter 16

## MYITKYINA & PINE VILLA                              1945

In June of 1945 the Japanese were driven from southern Burma. With that accomplished the 4th Combat Cargo group had served its purpose — The Burma war was ending. But the news from the Pacific war front was grim. To push the Japanese back, the Allies suffered excruciating losses. On Okinawa 12,000 Americans were killed, and 36,000 wounded; 150,000 Japanese were also killed.

In May, five square miles of Tokyo were obliterated and 36 hours later another 16 square miles destroyed. In June, 500 U.S. planes dropped 3,000 tons of fire bombs on Kobe but with no visible effects on Japanese resolve. On the contrary, in each case the Japanese had demonstrated they would not surrender but would fight to the death. The military in Washington were estimating that it would take between 500,000 and 1 million American lives to invade Japan and win.[1]

At home we knew nothing about the top secret effort to develop an atomic bomb. Were there rumors about such a bomb circulating among the men? I don't know, but if there were, I doubt that any would have voted against using it. Stories of the horrendous atrocities inflicted on the populations overrun by the Japanese were now circulating freely. There was little sympathy for the enemy; those of us at home wanted this brutal war to end in the quickest possible way.

At this point in June, Chick's group was divided up and moved one more time. Pilots and air personnel were assigned to the Air Transport command (ATC) to carry gasoline, troops, and supplies over the Hump into China. Some of the men were assigned to fly Chinese nationalist soldiers from Shanghai to be deployed against Chinese communists under the leadership of Mao Tse Tung. This was

---

1    facts from TRUMAN by David McCollough Simon & Schuster 1992

an unpopular mission. There was little to choose between the rampantly corrupt and decaying nationalist regime of Chiang Kai Shek and the equally dictatorial communist forces of Mao-Tse Tung. Caught in this Civil War after the Japanese had been routed from Shanghai, the American men wanted out. Few wished to risk their lives in the Chinese battle. Always an active anti-Communist, from his student days, Chick developed a deep rooted loathing toward the Chinese communists.

Along with his squadron Chick had moved from Sylhet to Agartala to Chittagong and now he was assigned to the base in Myitkyina, Burma, where he waited impatiently for the war to end.

Meanwhile, in the U.S., all through this period, fifty countries were engaged in working through the statement of principles for the charter of the future organization on world security. On June 27, 1945, the signing of the United Nations charter took place in San Francisco. From the outset of these meetings, both Chick and I were disillusioned by the reported squabbling and bickering over what seemed to us foolish matters in the face of men still giving their lives. The diplomatic methods were discouraging. Did it really matter who sat where at the San Francisco conference table? Clearly it did. The solution was the use of a round table. Struggling to get through the days, Chick was losing patience. The following letter reflects some of the anger he was feeling.

❖

8 June, 1945
India

Dearest Most Wonderful Darling,

Again this day went rather quickly. Once more I was deeply engrossed in work, classification at that, and I feel as tho I accomplished quite a bit. Everyone around feels as tho I'm at least an asset and we all get on fairly well together. Now more than ever, I don't find the time to do all the things I want to do. In writing yesterday's letter I wanted to write you about a number of things, but didn't get around to it. Before I get started on something else, I'd best get on with it.

You may truly feel the way you expressed yourself in 171, concerning my army service. Good for you. It's quite an idealistic approach with just enough realism to make it level headed. I wish I could feel that way. I felt as you did once — possibly even more so — but no longer. If I were a soldier during the American Revolution, I'd no doubt be a "summer soldier, a sunshine patriot." If I hadn't you, I could be happy here, or even at Okinawa. But you are real, not someone that is part of a mirage. My heartache is real, my longings and desires, more so. What is all of this, compared to them. How can anything in the world make up for these years torn from my life, torn out of my heart?

And, at those times, when a spark of idealism is rekindled, and I say that things don't come easy, they must be fought for and paid for and I'm doing both, paying for the wonderful future that is in store for both of us. When I think that, things are easier. But then the uncertainty of a future peaceful world arises, and I see that days pass without a solution or any progress toward one. When that occurs, I think back on all of this and say "What a fool I've been!" How simple it would have been to connive and outwit, to debase and deceive, to the end that I would be spared all this. Yes, I think that would have been best. This now is not my fight. Mine is one that will end in Peace. For generations and generations to come. This one thus far has destroyed one tyrant and will in time, destroy another. But the seeds for future discontent are being sown now. And the beautiful effort that had the beginnings of a new brotherhood, is now employed at sniping at one another, at questioning each others motives. Suspicion is now bred where trust once held sway. Such is the picture that unfolds before me now.

And then, in my personal relationships with the army, day after day, to do inconsequential tasks with little or no meaning. Day after day to spend hours in sheer boredom. Day after day to live but never to get any mental exercise. Rarely if ever to feel exhilarated and happy over the knowledge of worthwhile accomplishment. Can I ever expect you to visualize or understand all of this, if I couldn't, when I was back at Sedalia? Too many things must be experienced to be understood. Can you "feel real grief" until it strikes home? Can the human mind conceive of something that has a purely mental and nervous reaction?

How I loathe this existence! How day in, day out, I search for surcease, but very little of it comes. Oh yes - I'll get thru it all right. But the price I've paid. Will it be worth it? To those who are now dead because of it, no matter what the outcome, it could never have been worth their dying. My life has too great a price on it for anything in the world but you and Robert, to be worth it. And each day of it, each month, each year, is priceless too. Do I now exchange these for "Fool's Gold," for snide phrases of "Peace Brother," for "grasping nationalism, either British or Russian," for unemployment and poverty and general insecurity in the post war years. Is that the bargain I find myself making?

You may think now, that I shall feel good in future years, at the small part I played in this fight. Whenever, I shall in the future express myself thusly — you must know now, that it is not so. If I ever boast of "The CBI" it will be only that, and nothing more. Mere words that may serve to bolster my ego. I may only go out of my way at times, to make a point of "army service" only because there's a lucky bastard around who for one reason or another, didn't see any. Cruelly, I'll be taking some small revenge in making him uncomfortable. If I speak at all about my service, you can be sure that there will be some ulterior motive. Some self-seeking motive, nothing more.

Never, never, will I be proud of it. Never will even a glimmer of happiness come at the thought of it. It shall leave a long and bitter memory only. How long they shall remain with me, depends on how successful your "nursing" will be. What a grand joke Fate has played. Cast in the role of a "fighter for Freedom" I revile the Fight and regret bitterly, every day, every ounce of energy put into it. No, I'm here, and will sweat it out. But the Brass Bands and stupid sentiment shall be for other's ears. They can never assuage my hurt. They can never begin to repay, that way.

What I have written above, will provide the clues, as to why I don't write to MK [friend] or the others any more. I live in a world apart now. Most of the time I don't think

195

too clearly and have scant patience to "make phrases." I have disassociated myself from my former life. To write them is to once more become part of it and to feel the pangs of comparing it with this one. My only entree to it is you. You alone, of all that is in it, remain as fine and pure as always. You alone are life and love; hope and faith; you alone are my world. I cling and seek to hold you. For thru you alone can I learn to live again, to laugh again. You see sweetheart, I have made a world of my own here — separate and apart from the one I left not so long ago. Here, all is boredom, inaction, unreal, without love or beauty, ambition or ideals. With one exception, there is beauty only in thinking of you and dreaming of you. I ask for your pictures only to see you more clearly and to heighten the emotions. I write to you and unburden myself, and get relief that way. I am happy too, while writing, and that makes up for the drudgery that is each day. As long as I have your love, I can maintain that equilibrium. Your love has always been so important, but never so much as now.

I find tonite, that you may again be depressed at reading this. But I think by now, that you've come to expect these every now and then. And getting them, you take them at face value, and smile, knowing that the next day's letter will be a happy one and that what I write, at any one time, is not really indicative of a continuing state of mind.

So it goes. I got wound up tonite, and as a result, I leave you without talking about other items I wanted to. So it's your gain, for I shall write again in the morning. I appreciate your writing two letters in one day as you did on 28th May, but you had missed writing the day before. Is there any percentage in that?

Stay with me darling - when I get out of this rut — when I get this out of my system, I'll be back on the beam, talking sense, being more pleasant and generally, being a better person.

Bye now, for a few hours. These moments with you are treasured beyond all else. If you are not happy tonite because of this letter, you'll feel so much better tomorrow, with the next one.

I love you my darling. You are my life. How one person can be so utterly dependent upon another, as I am dependent upon you, is almost inconceivable. Stay well and keep happy.

Millions of kisses and caresses for you.

CHICK

❖

This deeply emotional letter expressed so much that Chick was unable to share with anyone else. I was struck by the depth of his anger and frustration, the power of his words, and the potential truth of his comments, especially, "the seeds for future discontent are being sown now." I labeled his letter "blue Monday," and decided that this was definitely one I wanted to keep.

It was now the last week in June, and time to head for the country. Robert, two and one half years old, was primed and ready. Chattering away, he joined in the preparations selecting books and toys while my mother and I agonized over what to pack. We would need warm clothes for cool summer nights, rain wear for summer storms, light shorts and halters for hot, humid days. Linens and towels were not provided there and even some kitchen utensils were needed — a small army unit on the move.

Packing was one thing, but with so many bags and boxes to carry, getting there was another. We hired a hacker — a man who owned and drove a livery-cab or jitney. The cars, always black, could seat five or six people and were fitted with a rack on the roof. Through June, and early July, hacks piled high with boxes, bicycles, over-stuffed luggage squeezed closed, tied with ropes and covered with a tarpaulin, could be seen clogging the roads upstate.

My father joined us for the trip. He planned to help us get settled, enjoy a bit of relaxation, then return home with the men. Having Grandpa along was a special treat for Robert, who clambered happily into the hack with him. My mother, father and I sat in the back, Robert chose a jump-seat. Prepared with games, books, and plenty of snacks and fruit, we were ready to roll.

The trip to Wurtsboro, New York, (about fifty-five miles from the Bronx) took almost five hours. Thousands were leaving the suffocating heat of New York's un-air-conditioned apartments. With no federal expressways to speed the ride, we traveled the crowded two-lane road bumper to bumper most of the way. We stopped for street lights in every town and Main Street, getting hotter and stickier as the day wore on. A few hours into the trip we took a pit stop and lunch break at the forerunner of fast food chains, The Red Apple Rest. (There, together with a hundred other frazzled travelers, we bought hamburgers and hot dogs with all the fixings, while gulping Dr. Peppers to cool us down.)

Without car air-conditioning on that stifling hot Burma-weather day, the trip tested our endurance and withered our enthusiasm as we listened to Robert's incessant questions, "Are we there? When we gonna get there? How much longer?" We distracted him with count-ing games, songs, and whatever stories we could make up about the people in other cars on the road. Finally, the motion of the car put him to sleep. Only the mileage signs told us we were making progress.

The sight of the lackluster sign, PINE VILLA brought me back to life. "That's us!" I announced.

As we pulled into a partly paved driveway, we could see a non-descript two story house straight ahead. Painted white, with a peaked roof and a plain front door, one saving grace caught my eye — there, along the entire front of the house was a terrific porch where children could play, rain or shine. A youngster was running up the few steps to the porch, excitedly announcing our arrival. Robert, who had jumped out of the car as soon as we stopped, started to move cautiously toward him. Just then a group of smiling people emerged from the house. We hardly had time to unstick our sweaty clothes from our backs and legs when we were surrounded with welcoming shouts and kisses.

They had arrived a day or two before, settled in, and looked like they had been vacationing for a month. Two were my parent's friends, the others were cousins, their married daughters, sons-in-law and several grandchildren. Altogether, we were five or six families. They bubbled with pleasure, pitched in to help us unload the hack, and once that was done, delighted us with refreshing iced tea drinks in tall glasses. I fell in love with the cousins and new family members I was meeting for the first time. Forgotten was the hot, boring ride; the prosaic farm house that promised little from its exterior had become a friendly home. I now understood why my mother had been so sure the summer would work out.

Our room was adequate, nothing fancy. A home-made dividing wall separated our sleeping quarters so that Robert and I could sleep in twin beds on one side of the partition, and my parents could have the double bed on the other, larger side. We each had a dresser and window, with flimsy white curtains and dark pull-down shades for privacy. On my parent's side, there was one closet, and a small sink that gave us access to the delicious well-water. This meant we could wash, brush our teeth as well as drink, without going to the bathroom across the hall. Through some cobwebbed mental image, I can see a small table and two chairs near the sink where we could sit to talk or read.

What I do remember very clearly, is not the room, but rather how wonderful it was that Robert could run free on his own outdoors. He made friends quickly with the other children, but was intrigued by the one infant whom he watched carefully and learned to rock gently in the carriage.

It was an ordinary place, no frills, no beautiful gardens, no flowers at all except for the wild varieties of Queen Anne's Lace and buttercups, that grew alongside the road. But there were easy trees to climb, a log fence low enough to sit on or scoot over, enough grassy places for sitting or playing, a large sand box for the children, and several good sized boulders scattered about that were made to order for me. Weathered smooth, they were grand to lie on when I wanted privacy — a place to be alone where I could see the dappled sunlight through the trees, smell the new-mown grass, and linger at night in reverie with the brilliant stars and sky, thinking of Chick, wondering — was he safe? What was he doing? When would I see him again? When would the war end? Was he writing poetry right now?

The communal kitchen worked out without a hitch; the women were easy-going, not a prima donna in the group. In one large room, each family had their own table and chairs, a small two-burner stove, a shelf for dishes, glasses, etc. and a cupboard to store provisions. I don't remember if we all shared one refrigerator or if there was more than one. Everyone prepared meals that required little cooking or fussing, and we all knew how to share. When an orange disappeared or if someone ate someone else's apple, it was simply a "so what" thing. No one raised a ruckus — after all, we weren't dealing with filet mignon or a fluffy soufflé! Robert sampled everyone's cooking, learning to eat things he would never have touched in other circumstances. My mother picked up some new recipes and shared a few of her own. In July we went huckleberry picking. Robert came back with blue fingers and a purple mouth, the rest of us returned with a full pail of berries. All week there were shared berry pies, cakes, muffins, plain berries and cream, and jam. Of course, a supply was set aside for the weekend when the men came.

It was a lazy summer, easy and pleasant. We took long walks into town to buy yarn for knitting, crocheting or embroidery. My mother's friends purchased fabrics which they cut and sewed into shorts, halters and rompers, all stitched by hand. We had a built-in sewing circle where jokes and stories were exchanged. My own nimble fingers were at work on a new sweater for Robert or gloves for the winter ahead. Hand work had always been a pleasurable activity at home, now it was more so. Mostly I recall the sounds of laughter, less often the scolding voice of mothers with children.

We were sheltered from the outside world. Only the farmer had a radio. We called him "the farmer," although nothing was grown on the property. It seemed he liked to be thought of as the farmer and not a landlord, just as we liked to think of the place as a farm, not a rooming house. Radio reception was very poor in the mountains and since there were no battery run radios, you could listen only indoors. We relied on newspapers for the war news and looked forward to the weekends and New York papers. We knew if something "big" happened we would hear about it.

When the men arrived Friday there was great rejoicing. It was a happy time with lots of hugging and kissing. Gifts were exchanged and the resounding male voices brought new life to the house. They were always particularly attentive to Robert, coming in with a gift for him, too. Occasionally, an argument erupted between a husband and wife, usually mediated quickly by the others. A simple, "What! You didn't come here to fight, you know," or "I thought you came to have a good time," did the trick.

My gift was always the letters my father brought from Chick. I had not changed my address for the summer fearing a letter might go astray somewhere in the Catskills. I loved to see the men and hear their stories of work and city problems, but it was their lives, not mine and I could not repress the stab of wanting.

While others chatted and caught up with the weekly stories, I would go to my flat rock and read my letters and poems. I read them over and over and over all week.

❖

To hold you again and once more whisper
Words of love. To see you before me, smiling,
With a laughing heart.
To be with you to
Share your joys and complete happiness.

To stroll again, upon the walks of yesteryear
Reawakening memories that time itself could
Not dull. And in strolling, then to plan
And plan, our future bright that will
In later years, supply more pleasant memories.

To play with Robert, our son, the product of
Our Love. To have him run to me, excitedly
Pointing to one of the many mysteries of life
About him. And you'd pick him up and hold
Him and I'd see my life before me.

These things all add up to your "Love"
I love you,
CHICK

❖

July disappeared in the way July always does - too fast - and it was August. Chick had been asking for new pictures of me, "Send some cheese-cake," he wrote. Laughingly, I mentioned it to the sewing circle. Bernice, the sixteen-year -old, spoke up. "If you have film, I know just how to take the kind of shots he wants." I changed into the satin shorts and taffeta blouse my mother had made for me, and posed as directed, "Stand on tip toe, reach as high as you can, now look at me and smile — great!" After several more poses we were done. I mailed them out labeled, "Cheese Cake for Chick."

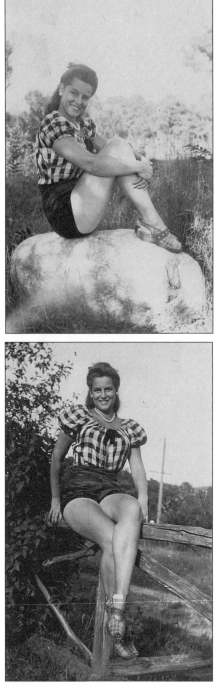

1945
Cheese Cake
for Chick

The New York Times
August 7, 1945
*Courtesy of The New York Times Co.*

The New York Times
August 9, 1945
*Courtesy of The New York Times Co.*

"All the News That's Fit to Print"

# The New York Times.

LATE CITY EDITION

VOL. XCIV No. 31,908     NEW YORK, WEDNESDAY, AUGUST 15, 1945     THREE CENTS

# JAPAN SURRENDERS, END OF WAR!
# EMPEROR ACCEPTS ALLIED RULE;
# M'ARTHUR SUPREME COMMANDER;
# OUR MANPOWER CURBS VOIDED

**RING MADE LOCAL**

Communities, Labor and Management Will Unite Efforts

**___,000 AFFECTED**

Draft Quotas Cut, Services to Drop 5,500,000 in 18 Months

**Third Fleet Fells 5 Planes Since End**

**ALL CITY LETS GO**

Hundreds of Thousands Roar Joy After Victory Flash Is Received

**TIMES SQ. IS JAMMED**

Police Estimate Crowd in Area at 2,000,000—Din Overwhelming

**SECRETS OF RADAR GIVEN TO WORLD**

Its Role in War and Uses for Peacetime Revealed at Washington and London

PRESIDENT ANNOUNCING SURRENDER OF JAPAN

Mr. Truman reading the message to War

**PETAIN CONVICTED, SENTENCED TO DIE**

**Terms Will Reduce Japan To Kingdom Perry Visited**

**TREATY WITH CHINA SIGNED IN MOSCOW**

Complete Agreement Reached With Chungking on All Points, at Issue, Romans Say

### World News Summarized

WEDNESDAY, AUGUST 15, 1945

**YIELDING UNQUALIFIED, TRUMAN SAYS**

Japan Is Told to Order End of Hostilities, Notify Allied Supreme Commander and Send Emissaries to Him

**MACARTHUR TO RECEIVE SURRENDER**

Formal Proclamation of V-J Day Awaits Signing of Those Articles—Cease-Fire Order Given to the Allied Forces

By ARTHUR KROCK

Orders Given to the Japanese

**Cruiser Sank, 1,196 Casualties;**
**Took Atom Bomb Cargo to Guam**

**MacArthur Begins Orders to Hirohito**

**Hirohito on Radio; Minister Ends Life**

**Two-Day Holiday Is Proclaimed; Stores, Banks Close Here Today**

The New York Times
August 15, 1945
*Courtesy of The New York Times Co.*

Chapter 17

## "WAR ENDS IN A RAIN OF RUIN"                    1945

The announcement of the first atom bomb dropped on Hiroshima, August 6, 1945, sent waves of exhilaration through me, followed by tremors of uncontrollable fear, as everyone at Pine Villa rushed to hug and kiss one another, crying, "The war is over! It's over! Chick will be coming home now." Of course the Japanese had not yet surrendered, but the commentators on the radio seemed to take it for granted that this bomb left the enemy no choice. Our friends at Pine Villa treated the news as an end to the fighting. Unlike the muted celebrations at the end of the war in Europe, joyous peals of laughter and unrestrained whoops of happiness erupted. My trembling gave way to a numbing sensation in my head. Robert was jumping and laughing as women tossed him joyously, sing-songing his daddy was coming home now.

I took him up to our room where we could talk. Yes, his dad would be coming home, but we did not know exactly when. We would still have to wait patiently. We looked at Chick's pictures and talked about him a bit, as we often did together. He said he wanted his dad to come soon he wanted him to come now.

As the days passed my fears persisted. The people around me just weren't thinking. Wars didn't end that way — drop a bomb and poof, it's over! There were still so many questions to be answered. Would the Japanese surrender or continue to fight. Every day, we heard more about this secret weapon. Days passed and still there was no surrender. Three days later a second bomb was dropped and Russia entered the fight. My fears rode me like a roller coaster. When would the surrender come? Without that, the war would continue and men would die. Even after surrender, would soldiers be kept overseas for an extended time because of the Chinese communist card in play now? And what about this bomb, what did that mean? The nagging, underlying panic was telling me that nothing was over until it was over. Men and women continue to be injured, even killed in the armed forces after hostilities cease. You could count on more than a few human interest stories to appear reporting mistakes, accidents, or foolish tricks that snuff out lives randomly. We were so close to the end. Would we really make it through the remaining dangers that lay ahead? No one in our group seemed to be thinking these thoughts.

When the Japanese surrendered on August 14, I knew only the first step had been taken before my life could be whole again. The next months would be difficult, but we had come too far not to feel optimistic about the future.

The weeks that followed were the most unsettling of all the war days. My thoughts ran in circles. "What did it mean for us? There were accidents, anything could happen. Would they demobilize quickly? No, it would take forever. Was there a plan, or would Chick be stranded for months? Yes, surely it would take months before he'd be released. Did I have the strength for the waiting now? Of course, it's so close. What did it mean for us?..."

What was Chick thinking, I wondered. If only I could call him, tell him to be more careful. But, I'd never say that. He needed optimism from me, expressions of "this is it, it can't be too long now," not fear and apprehension, not negative thoughts of the evils that lurk around dark corners. Ordinarily it would take two weeks before I would hear from him about his reactions and feelings to an event. This time it took much longer. He sent a "short jumbled" note saying that he was at the teletype when the message of the atom bomb explosion came over. Although I saved it, that note has disappeared. He had added "It's all over now!" and then I waited and waited before I received the letters that follow — letters that show he was echoing the same strains as I — both of us afraid to allow full reign to our longings, dreams and prayers. Even the poems slowed almost to a halt.

❖

14 Aug. 1945 Burma

Dearest Sweetest Rosalind:

It is really the 15th now and just a few moments ago news of Japanese surrender came to us. It seems to be really over at last. It is virtually impossible to describe my emotions and reactions of the past three or four days. I hope the lack of mail from me didn't unnerve or upset you. You see, I didn't write, since that short jumbled letter several days ago when news of the Jap surrender offer got to us. That is inexplicable in and of itself. And yesterday was the first sleep I've had in three days and tonite again, no sleep for here it is about five AM and I haven't been to bed yet. I shan't go either until I finish this letter.

To begin with, the surrender offer found me with a "wet" cough and a sniffy nose. That evening the place went wild. Every day room was well stocked with liquor and it flowed freely. The authorities showed foresight in that all personnel were directed to turn in their weapons. As it was, hundred of colored flares were shot off, making for a brilliant sky. And the ack ack boys, really let go with their guns. When I get home, I'll describe it to you in detail. It was a scene probably repeated everywhere in this part of the world. And the same wild elation was present as must have been everywhere.

The first nite the news came, I was feeling kind of rough and because of the cold, I couldn't celebrate properly at all. I did manage to down about two drinks, and sat around with some of the more sober ones and talked until about 2 AM. I really felt tired and headed for the sack, hoping and expecting to fall asleep. But no dice. The moment I hit the sack, my brain began whirling and grinding away on all two cylinders. A fast kaleidoscopic review of events of the past few years paraded by. All my thoughts were mumbled and jumbled, some sane, some wild indeed. I tried to relax, but couldn't . A little while later, dawn came and with it, some quiet thoughts of you. Then the next day, in the PM, some of the boys resumed their celebration, but I was feeling miserably lousy for by this time the old nose was really running and I had a horrible headache. I couldn't think or write, or talk. I had rubbed my nose raw and taken more pills than Carter ever had. I sat down to write, after chow on the 11th but couldn't get past the salutation. All I could think of was 'I'm coming home — it won't be long." But I was afraid to write even that. What if somehow the war was prolonged (How I prayed for its end)? So I laid the paper aside and went to the Day Room to listen to the news. There was little but rumor.

In a little while a card game started and I thought I'd do well to play and try to take my mind off the misery of my cold and the uncertainty of whether or not all that we've been praying for would come thru.

It was a small game, two rupee limit, and we played on and on. Between hands I sneezed and coughed and blew my nose, but I managed to keep interested and I won about 100 rupees. We quit late, about 3:00 AM, and the moment we did so, I felt that old confusion and wondering returning. I felt "excited" and not calmed as when I was gambling.

Again I couldn't sleep at all the rest of the nite, and the next day dog tired I made my bleary eyed way to my desk. And most of the day I weathered thru some reports and managed to keep going. After chow in the evening, I made my way to the Day Room again. It was now the 13th and news would surely be forthcoming. I tried to write again, but words refused to come! I couldn't write until I knew definitely one way or another. As I sat there, I felt pretty good. Sort of tired, yes — and I wondered how come I didn't fall asleep in the chair. But my cold felt much better and I guess I was too tired to be tired. So when another poker game started I played too. This was for bigger stakes and again I was lucky and won about 300 Rs.

About 12:30 I felt my eyes closing upon me and a headache coming up. Two of the fellows, knowing of my cold urged me to quit and I did. I came to the sack, and wondered whether I'd sleep this nite. God, "I'd bombed Hell out of Japan in my thoughts for two nites running, and have flown over the oceans to be at your side, so many times." Could I sleep tonite? I did! All I remembered was seeing Bassett at 8 PM ready to go to work and the next thing I knew, it was 14 Aug., 11 AM. I was dead to the world — so sound asleep. All afternoon this place was electric with rumor. The answer would come today! It was on its way to Washington! That's all we did was to sit around and speculate. And when 5:30 PM rolled around, many of us were losing hope! I sat down on the sack and decided to wait for Bassett so we could go to chow, and again the next thing I knew was that a light was shining in my eyes. Hank, one of the others in the tent was there, saying "How the hell could anyone sleep so soundly thru the noise we made?"

"Is the war over" I asked?

"Hell no — we were just drinking some beer."

"What time is it," I asked as I noticed the darkness about us.

"9:30, time to listen to the news." I was pretty hungry too and really wide awake by now. So I went to the Day Room and sat around, ears glued to the radio and eating some sandwiches and having a few drinks. About 11 PM an announcement came that the Jap reply was on its way to Washington. Then and there, a few of us decided to wait for the news even if it took 24 hrs. We wouldn't budge we promised ourselves. Just in case we should fall asleep, I called the C.Q., told him we were at the day room and that he should come over at 5 PM and wake us in time for the 5:15 news. Then we talked again about a million things until one by one, the four of us fell asleep sprawled in these easy chairs that we have.

At 5:00 we were awakened and a few moments later, the news came. It was over! We could do nothing else but heave a sigh of relief — mutter the fervent wish that we could soon start our trip home — and walk to our tents! It was raining and I braced up enough to shake the cobwebs from my brain. I decided to write now — as soon as I could before I hit the sack — for I knew that I'd sleep for days now. It was over. Maybe I could feel relaxed once again..

That was it. Four nites and days — fateful — yet meaningless to me. All of them were telescoped into one long stretch. Nite was day and day was nite for me! All I did was gamble, sit around, work a little and sleep less. And all I could think of was — How much I loved you — How desperately I wanted this to end — How fervently I wanted to start on my way to you now.

I started to write many times dearest. I wanted to say something, anything, but I couldn't. Try to forgive me darling, I haven't written the folks either for a week. I got 5 letters from you the last 4 days too and they were wonderful. I'm going to bed now and I shall re-read everyone of them and write in the evening, tonite. I've almost fallen asleep over this letter sweetheart. I must go now.

Oh dearest adorable Rosalind, Lovely wonderful wife. The war is over! If we're lucky I'll be home about Christmas time. What a wonderful dream come true that will be. Maybe in a few weeks we'll learn what will happen to this group.

I love you dearest , I love you, love you, love you. With all my heart, my soul, my life itself. I am yours alone, every part of me always and Forever I love you, adore you, worship you!!

I love you so, only you, I love you<br>
CHICK

16 Aug. 45

Dearest Darling Ros:

I don't know how to ask you to forgive me sweetheart. If only I could master the adequate words to explain the confusion and turmoil that raced thru my consciousness, this past week, If only I could somehow recapture the past few days and write you those long letters that should have been written, but weren't.

All thru this hectic period, thru every moment of it, I was aware only of my deep love for you, of my intense longing and wild desire to be with you, to share the wonderful news that I knew somehow, was forthcoming. And as the moment came when we realized that it was over now, I faced it with mixed emotion. Was the war really over for me, and you? No — it wouldn't be over until we were together. For millions of others, the world over, it would be.

But Myitkyina was still a terribly long way from Life — from you and our Love. And somehow I'm pessimistic enough to believe that this process of repatriating GI's will be a painfully slow one. So for days I existed almost entirely oblivious to things around. I was afraid to even think of leaving for the States within a month or so. Too afraid to think of being with you, to celebrate Robert's third birthday. I was up whole days and nites at a time, running the gamut of emotions from gleeful optimism to glum pessimism. And all the hours were sped along, talking, drinking and playing cards.

I wanted to write, God knows my darling, I tried to write. I could hold the pen, but the words couldn't come. I could think of nothing to say coherently. I could only repeat what my heart pounded out. I love you, I love you. And now I find that if I couldn't write more than that, I should at least have said that. Constantly, my thought were of you. Several times during these sleepless nites, I'd be sitting around and I'd be so, so engrossed in our love, that I'd kiss you in thought and it felt so real so thrilling. I'd hold you close and could actually feel your body, warm and desirous so a part of me. It was real. I jumped up with a start and it was still Myitkyina and I was still alone, and so terribly lonely.

And all thru this period your letters were coming thru beautifully and I tried to answer them and so insure a steady stream of letters to you. Over and over I'd read them, smilingly, hopefully praying for the second miracle that would have to be wrought so that you and I could be together soon.

All these long months of separation, all these longer months of living a nomadic existence — were they to end soon - abruptly, gloriously — in those first moments of reunion. They certainly would — for I'd never leave you never, never.

Even now, when by all that is reason, I should now be somewhat calmed, all I can think of is getting home to you. Nothing else matters in the least. I want to tell you of my love, to pledge it anew. I want to take hold of the words and have them pour forth I want to. I must!!

From that very first day when my love for you found itself some 6 ½ yrs ago, from that day onward it has grown and flowered and matured — deeply, sincerely and passionately. And that little flame that your loveliness and charm kindled then has grown until its fire consumes my being. I love you Rosalind, more than life itself and without your Love there would be no Life for me. Every fond wish, every kind hope is of you alone. Every moment is spent planning for your happiness and dreaming of our wonderful life together.

These next months will be really desperate ones. How near we are to each other and yet how far. Now more than ever, our love for each other must bid us be patient. Now more than ever, will we dream these dreams of love and beauty, for they are so close to fulfillment. I'll be back soon. It may yet be six months, possibly less, but it will be sooner than we dared hope before. Realizing that, perhaps then time won't hang as heavy as before.

I love you Rosalind. Adorable wonderful wife — my sweetest dearest love. With all my heart and mind - with all the strength and fire within me with all the wild hopes that are products of my unbridled desire, I want you near - to kiss you, fondle you, play with you, speak with you. I want to share the thrill of raising Robert, and of bringing him brothers or sisters. I want the joy of planning and building a home for us. I want these and more and want them so desperately. Above all, I want you, need you so very much. And yet, tho these days and nites be so lonely, we must as always put one foot after another, hoping, as we have always hoped that the last step will be taken a lot sooner than we thought it might.

The prospect of staying on in the CBI for 5 or 6 months more, is hateful, but understandable. If we remain in Myitkyina, it will be criminal. I was always afraid of being caught overseas when the war ended. Here we are now. They will no doubt want this group to do a lot of hauling of supplies to seaports so they can be taken back to the states. They don't give much of a damn for humans. If they did they could clear the CBI of all Yanks in 3 months. There aren't many of us here, in the world's worst areas.

The hell with the bastards — let them do their worst. I begrudge them each passing day but I know it will be over and done with soon, and our reunion will serve to blot out the distaste and hate and sorrow that these months will bring.

Stay well dearest. I promise longer and more interesting letters from now on. I'm back in stride and I'll try so hard to make up for this past week. I love you so, dearest Rosalind — so very much! You are all my life. I love only you —

CHICK

❖

As we reached the end of August, we were approaching our fifth wedding anniversary. Still in our twenties, Chick was 27 and I was 22. My thoughts flitted from passionate week-ends and school vacations with summers of music, to joyful months in Massachusetts and Missouri. I tried to figure the actual days we'd spent together. The best I could come up with was two years out of five. Not much of a record, I thought, but still far luckier than many, many others. The future held so much promise now. I wrote Chick of my memories, linking my heart to all his longings, and imagining a life ahead free of intrusion, free to make our own choices. He too was remembering and writing of our anniversary.

❖

22 Aug 45
Burma

Dearest Darling Rosalind:

Another day crossed off the calendar and there was little to recommend it but the fact that I did get two letters from you, 244, and 245. All of this after I was fairly certain that I wouldn't get any. I can enjoy being pleasantly surprised like this any time at all!

Yesterday I wanted to talk about something you wrote in 243. You were wondering aloud at what my reactions would be, if you thought you'd want something, or want to do something and I thought differently. You said "There would be nothing I'd want that you'd deny me — that is nothing within reason." Well you're right. Right now the uppermost thought, the fondest wish that I have, is for your happiness. I love you so deeply my darling, that even a slight preference on your part would be sufficient. It wasn't always that way — not because I loved you less three years ago — only because I've acquired a different perspective since then. Only because now some things that mattered then are less important now. It was "cute" then to make each decision an exercise in logic, and more often than not I figured I was right. But that is gone by the board now. You are brighter now than I am, and then your personal happiness is of greater importance to me, than my being "right."

Yes sweetheart — I'd rather be happy than right, and I'd rather be right than be president. In these lovely years to come then, I'll try to work on this. Yet there will no doubt be some times when "you'll have to convince me!" Yet these too will only be few and far between. A sweet smile from you on those occasions would no doubt dissolve my opposition and crumple my defenses. How anxiously I join with you in awaiting those wonderful days and years that will make a lifetime of love for both of us.

In a few days we shall have been married five years. That's such an artificial date, 31 Aug. I say that for we were wedded so fully when we first exchanged our love. When we first pledged our hearts to each other. Now these past years with their many memories are indelibly engraved on my memory. They were such lovely ones. If only I could think of some sweet things to say — some wondrous song to sing. But my heart and mind are doing just that as I write. Can you hear them? Over and over, again and again, they pledge my love, so full, so devoted, so sincere. I wanted to send something for you. I thought perhaps I'd go to Kunming to find a gift, but there was little opportunity. Yet you must know that any gift, no matter how worthwhile would pale into insignificance in comparison with the love and the life that I offer.

Five years — such a short time, and yet they have brought so much to us. How much sweeter and richer the next 5 and the next 50, will be. I love you so, Ros. Happy Anniversary, adorable wife.

These letters which came today were written on the 10th and 11th. I can't help but think that just about now, you've been sweating out letters from me and none were coming for several days. I regret that yet, a great deal!

The first intimation as to the end of the war came to you that morning as you were roused out of bed. Here, since the very first news of the Atomic Bomb came to us, I told the gang it was "all over." And during those uncertain days it was I who steadfastly maintained it was just about over and done with. During this one period from the 10th to the 15th there was a spontaneous demonstration only that nite when they shot off the ack ack and fellows were so joyful. They couldn't contain themselves. It was a wearing period and the acceptance of surrender terms found everyone too exhausted mentally and physically too — to do much other than smile wanly and demonstrate weakly. We all knew that the "Big Sweat" was on. But there was life in us for our eyes sparkled with rekindled dreams of home. We'd get there soon 4 months, 6 months, 9 months, what matter — the war was over; the butchery gone and done with. It wouldn't be long now, before we began to live once again.

I think the folks back home celebrated to a much greater extent. Surely the end of the war means almost as much to them as to the boys who daily faced it as a living reality. Yet when the first reports came that 65% of the civilians were opposed to acceptance of Japan's first surrender offer, never were army personnel so embittered against a civilian population. If lives were lost needlessly as a result of this "public opinion," a real hatred would spring up.

In my own mind, the original Jap offer was "unconditional" and not at all different from the terms now agreed upon. The mere acceptance by the Japs of "armed occupation" is full and complete surrender. Everything else is unimportant. Would they be in a position to do anything if subsequently we were to decide that the Mikado's death would be to our best interests and that of the Japanese themselves?

A defeated nation can have no safeguards other than the conscience of the victor. They surrendered on the 10th and only political maneuvering on their part and ours postponed acceptance until the 15th. Neither side was at all prepared for this sudden outcome. As I write, McArthur is planning to start the occupation about the the end of the month. Now they say that formal signing of the armistice will take place on the 31st. For us that date will have only a secondary meaning. That date will always remind us of that happy day 5 years ago.

The pictures you sent in 244 were lovely. You look a lot different in most of the shots you've sent since I was overseas. You look really healthy and lovely on these. Maybe it's your hair-do and shiny nose that always makes for these little differences. Certainly you are beautiful and wonderfully formed. I'm so very proud of you and so happy to be able to look at these! By the way, are these all you've been able to salvage out of those rolls of film?

Well, it's pretty late now and I've got to hit the hay. The days are going by and we're all just sweating out the High command's whim to move us. But we all feel confident that it will not be later than Easter — and probably Christmas. Doesn't that sound great!

I think of you more now than ever, if that's possible. We are closer together now than at any time these past two years. In a matter of months we'll be together again, this time for all time. I love you so — my darling. So very,very much. You are all my life, my hopes and desires. I love only you. I love you so.

CHICK

❖

When Chick had written on August 16th, "Every moment is spent planning for your happiness," I couldn't resist teasing him. "I must assume that there would be nothing I'd want that you'd deny me— that is, nothing within reason." Years later when I dug out this letter in an attempt to challenge a stubborn position, he waved his hand in a characteristic flippant gesture, laughed and said, "Now, you know I was out of my mind when I wrote that." Since that was true enough, I fell back to convincing him in the usual way, with humor and impeccable logic, not always in that order.

MONGOLIA

U.S.S.R.

YOKOTA  Oct. 1945
Jan. 1946

Peking

KOREA          JAPAN

CHINA

Seoul          Tokyo

Nanking

Shanghi

TACHIKAWA  Oct. 1945
Jan. 1946

Chunking

BOLO POINT  Aug. 1945
Sept. 1945

Kweilin

Okinawa

Kunming    Liuchow

Iwo Jima

Hong
Kong

FORMOSA

PACIFIC OCEAN

THAILAND

MARIANAS
ISLANDS

PHILIPPINE
ISLANDS

INDOCHINA

Guam

LEYTE  May - July 1945

MALAY
PENINSULA

SARAWAK

BIAK ISLAND  Dec. 1944
May 1945

Singapore

BORNEO

SUMATRA

JAVA

NEW
GUINEA

Batavia

INDIAN OCEAN

AUSTRALIA

Darwin

BASES OF THE
2ND COMBAT CARGO GROUP
1944 - 1946

# Chapter 18

## SHANGHAI                                                    1945

I did not know that as late as September 8th, some Japanese troops in Burma were still unaware of the August 15th surrender in Tokyo. Raiding parties continued along with resistance north of Rangoon. Three hundred Japanese, trapped in South Burma, refused to surrender and fired on Allied parties who approached under a white flag. The Burmese surrender was finally signed on September 14th and even then, some groups held out as late as September 26th, when they surrendered to the British.

Since we at home didn't hear or read about these incidents, I was looking ahead to demobilization, and worrying about how I could find a place of our own. I had nightmares of being stuck in the three room apartment when Chick returned. Enlisted men would be released in droves and the apartment crunch would surely worsen. I was compulsive about getting back from the country and went about alerting every friend and neighbor to be on the lookout for an available place. I began my own search through newspaper ads and introduced myself to apartment house superintendents for several frustrating weeks. They were not helpful; many were surly and downright rude.

One magical day, my dear friends Rebecca and Morris called to say they had found a larger place for themselves and their studio apartment would be available before the end of the year. How lucky could I get — it was the ideal place! Located in my parent's building, I could easily leave Robert with my mother, take the elevator down at will, night or day, and spend all the time I needed to move in. Yes, yes, good things were happening already, life was really turning around. It exhilarated and terrified me in equal amounts. I am not superstitious, but this was too easy and too good to be true.

In Burma meanwhile, as soon as the Japanese surrendered, many military units began folding. Throughout the area GIs began counting their service points, which were the demobilization credits the men

223

received for time served. Servicemen with the highest number of points would be discharged first. With little or nothing to do, some of the men in India held meetings to protest being kept overseas any longer.

At Myitkyina, where Chick was stationed, the men were bored and restless. In response, the army offered classes on a variety of subjects. Chick was asked to lecture on Labor Relations. He wrote about enjoying the hours he spent at the school. He seemed to be finding his voice as he lectured on collective bargaining, employer-employee relationships, social unionism, and other related labor topics. The classes stimulated lively discussions among the men, who were eager to talk about events and problems unrelated to war or demobilization points.

Chick filled the long tedious evenings playing poker with the men. He did handsomely well and I was delighted to receive his winnings in regular money orders each week — perfect timing to pay for all the purchases I made to furnish our apartment.

At the base any event became an excuse to party. They were over-supplied with the best scotch and Canadian whiskey, and with nothing left to do most of the day, cards and drinking took over. In this next letter, Chick writes about men with over seventy-five points who were getting ready to depart. What a wonderful reason to party!

❖

7 Oct. 45
Burma

Dearest Sweetest Rosalind:

Since I wrote yesterday quite a number of things, mostly of the pleasant variety occurred in this neck of the woods. Last nite, I wrote, and then ran over to the Day Room, where preparations for the party were being made. I was there only a little while and left for school where I lectured for only 1 ½ hrs; and then returned to the scene of the projected crime.

The boys were really in the process of tying one on. I immediately had a drink thrust upon me and I made a mental note not to drink more than three. As time went on, and I floated around from one little group to another, the realization came that this was one of the nicest male parties I'd every been at. Little choral groups of from 3 to 8 were settled in corners, singing all kinds of songs. One of the boys, Leon Weisfeld, had something of a kind of piano accordion, and he played all nite aided and abetted by fellows who got "sweet potato flutes" and just blew.

Whatever conversation there was, was alive and friendly and just damn good fun. And during the course of the first few hours, I managed to drink almost constantly — sipping highballs. Many of the fellows were happy drunk, and those that passed out were carried gently to their beds by three non-drinkers who took that job upon themselves. At about midnite or so, after a few quick drinks, I too became quite unsteady and joined a choral group and we sang everything from the "International" to "Jeannie with the Light...," and "Laura." It seems that all night long I'd been humming that tune and then we must have sung it many times.

About one o'clock, getting sleepier and hazier all the time, I decided to look for Bassett, who was half drunk when I had arrived after school. I was joined by two fellows more drunk than I and then we proceeded to look up and down the drainage ditches. No Bassett! We headed for the tent, and low and behold — Bassett, sprawled out in the sack.

We woke him and for 20 minutes we had a hell of a good time and I felt I was getting drunker by the minute.

Finally I got my clothes off, and kicked the others out, turned off the lights, got to the sack and flopped in. Immediately, the room started to twist and turn as tho it were a C-46 in a "thunderhead." It was really brutal. How long I lay thus, trying to anchor the ceiling down, I don't know. But I awoke this morning with a head that housed the whole damn Riveters Union. They surely pounded hell out of me, too. Bassett and I went over to the Medics and got a "remedy" and for the rest of the day, up until now, we've been quite subdued. Matter of fact, most of the fellows were "casualties" last nite and looked it all day today.

We've also been busy as hell all day getting everything straight for the departure tomorrow of these lucky 75 pointers etc. Incidently, you will probably get a call from one or two of them. Leon, and possibly a fellow, little fellow — so high ‡ Abe Weinberger. They'll say hello for me and tell you I'll be along in a couple of months. They should be in the states by Dec. 1. If I'm lucky now, I should make it about Jan 1 to 10th. It all depends on when they start shipping the 60 pointers out.

There are quite a few of us around and they may not get to the 61 pointers til the end of Nov. Then you've got to figure about 45 days from the time I leave this place till I get home. They are sending these men in this manner (1) Myitkyina to Chabua by plane - 45 min. (2) Processed there 3-4 days (3) Chabua to Karachi by train - 8 days and nites. (If by plane - 1 day about 8-9 hours) (4) Processing and awaiting embarkation - (up to 15 days etc. (5) Boat ride about 21 days. Schedule, about 48 days or so!!

It may be, that you will get a letter from me, saying I've left Myitkyina before Leon calls you! I sincerely hope so!

This is the first really big shipment of men aside from a few of our ships that flew to Shanghai. Nothing is being done now. And I doubt whether anything at all will be done any more. Not unless they ship in 500 new pilots or crew members. What the hell — so I'll lay around in Bed!

Darling, the first week of Oct. is over, and time really counts now. Let's keep pushing these days behind us dearest. Wishes and hopes have a way of coming true and "more things are wrought by prayer than this world dreams of."

I love you so, dearest Sweetest wife. I love you with all my heart, I adore you and worship you with each waking moment. Soon now darling — only a few steps, a few days, till we love again, live once again. I love you so.

CHICK

❖

Before the army years neither Chick nor I ever set time aside for a drink. Occasionally, on a Saturday night out, we would each order a highball. It made me sleepy and made Chick grimace. But everyone we knew enjoyed drinking, it seemed to make the evening more festive. Maybe it was like olives, I thought, you had to develop a taste for it. In time Chick's grimace disappeared, but I ultimately gave up drinking entirely when I went from getting sleepy to getting an asthma attack. That did it.

In Burma, they were sent the finest Scotch whiskey and Canadian rye. Liquor was readily available after working hours and Chick began to enjoy a drink or two with friends. In general, he said he avoided the booze-scene. He found greater pleasure in the many hours spent writing these wonderful letters, allowing his mind to float into the reveries that created poetry. Here, most of the letter is gone but the poem still kindles my spirit and keeps me warm.

❖

...It was so satisfying. I try to recall now exact phrases and images which formed in my mind, but I'm hard put to do so. The effect was so pleasant, so mellow, so contentedly relaxing. Just like I used to feel, when I'd embrace you, when I'd awake, finding you by my side - So warming and delightful. I grope for words to tell you of it, and of my love for you. If I sit still for a few moments, will they occur to me?

Have you ever felt that you must speak
So that others may share the joy you feel?
And then to your dismay to become meek
Or shy, or unable to express those feelings so real?

In response to a question asked of you,
Whose answer was simple, did you start to "say"
and suddenly stop, for tho the thoughts so true
Were there, the words that fitted them had flown away?

So it is with me. They ask, "Is your love so fair?"
And I smile and see your lovely face,
But the words are slow to come, and I wonder where
They went. Have they left me for another dwelling place?

At last, I see; I should have known
The course they took, so swift and straight and true,
To journey's end, your heart, there they have flown
Bringing with them my love, alone, for you!

Think of those moments, and you will know how I felt. Happy in these thoughts of you, I spend each passing day. Tho they are dreary and all consolation is lacking from them, there's always that glow that comes, when you "arrive."

I love you in so many ways. Each thought, each hope, each dream is you. No claim upon my heart can be made by any, for you have it. No one can call any part of me their own, for you have my body, my being! Each kiss, each caress, every tender embrace has been and always shall be, for you alone.

I love you, Rosalind — so very much. One day, not too many months from now, my actions, my life, will tell you what my words cannot.

Stay well my love, with my love for you alone, I love you, I love you, my own.

CHICK

❖

Without warning, without even a hint of any plan at all, letters from Shanghai arrived in a clump.

❖

10 Oct. 45<br>En route to a vacation

Dearest Darling Ros:

You may recall how many times I've threatened to visit either Calcutta or Kunming, and how those trips never did materialize? Ha - well - this is it. We are now at 12,000 ft.

Crossing the Hump into China, and of all places, on our way to Shanghai.

This month, after playing some poker and collecting some debts, I found myself quite rich. I sent you 25.00 and thought of sending more today when Major Hubka came into the orderly room and casually announced that he and Major Ehrhardt, the C.O. of the 13th Sq. were taking a trip to Shanghai. As I looked up, he asked if I wanted to go along. I nodded and told him there would be another passenger and he said OK. The other fellow was one who wanted to go to Kashmir with me on a furlough. He's a bright fellow from Chicago, a Jewish lad, and damn good company.

I called him — we packed and at 3:30 PM, we were at the plane waiting. Hubka told me that he'd be gone about 5 days. He had heard of wonderful Shanghai, and he had great expectations. I have too. Good food, nice place to stay and some interesting sight seeing. We took off at about 4 PM and in about ten minutes we landed at the North Strip. It seems as tho we have to take a jeep to Shanghai. That's the official reason for the trip. What a joke! The jeep is a wreck and should be junked in Burma. But here we're flying it about 1600 or more miles to be junked there. It's quite a neat trick, getting a jeep on board a C-46. Someday I'll tell you how it's done.

Just refilling my pen, Hubka came back to tell us he was going to land. It's very dark out, but below in the distance, I can see lights — Must be the runway. Our radio is in touch with the field, I can hear the landing instructions over the navigator's headset. We're dropping down now.

Best I put this away now. Be with you soon darling — soon as I get a bed for tonite!

Luliang, China

Here we are now. It's cooler here than at Myitkyina. I am seated at the ATC coffee shop with Marty Gertler waiting for coffee. Here there are a very limited number of cups and one has to wait until someone else finishes. So out with the letter! For the first time in months we've just finished eating "real eggs and potatoes." This trip already has an auspicious beginning.

Marty and I checked in at billeting and were given 4 blankets and a bed assignment. Seems they're quite crowded here — for others too are on their way to Shanghai. Just across from us are 4 men en route from a depot in India — newly arrived overseas. Average no. of pts. = 22 or so. When the hell will they get home? They're lucky at that, they are probably going to be based in Shanghai. Seems like all the headquarters are going to be established there.

There was an article in the army paper to the effect that little mail will now be flown to the States. Air traffic will be used almost exclusively for emergency travel, etc. So if these letters and those before it go by boat, they take 30 days to get to you. God!!

I still get letters from you in 9 to 11 days. They are so wonderful, I shall miss them so this next week.

Stay well — dearest Darling love — You have all of me, always and Forever. I love only you - I adore you - love you, only you, so very much!

CHICK

11 Oct. 45
Shanghai

Dearest Darling Ros:

Here we are — Shanghai. We took off from Luliang at about 5:30 AM after being awakened at about 4 AM. What a nite! If I got more than 2 hrs. sleep then I got a great deal. The bed was really rough and it was cold to boot. I don't know what I'll do in New York when I get home, especially if I'm lucky enough to be with you in January. I'll have to stay in bed all day and nite and you'll have to be right there along with me.

Well, we flew for about two hours and stopped at Chihkiang where we were supposed to pick up another jeep, but it was called off. So we decided to eat again and once more we ate those eggs and pancakes and they were really delicious. At 9 o'clock, we were gassed up and ready for Shanghai.

For almost 5 hours we flew across China, large, seemingly unending. Large mountains, uninhabited valleys, dry river beds, that's all there was until after several hours we burst in on the Yellow River Plain. This must be a very fertile valley for all the fields below looked well cultivated. Now and then, below us we could see clumps of houses, villages, towns. Shanghai was not far away - there it is! And as soon as you could make out the outlines of the city, you could also tell that the Navy was in! Ships of the 7th US Fleet just filled the harbor and many lay just offshore! We knew then that Shanghai was full of sailors. We circled the city just to give it the once over, and confirmed our hopes that this was quite a big place. Then to the airport.

Upon landing, we were amazed at the large number of American transport planes lined up! The 3rd group is now based here. They left Myitkyina about a week ago, but in addition ATC has hundred of others here. And many 4th group ships are here too. Like us. They have a little business to perform and are staying on for some recreation.

No sooner had the plane landed than we grabbed our bags and jumped out. We spoke to the Major for a few minutes and made a tentative appointment to meet in town. We flagged a jeep and got a ride to the ATC office. There we found that our passes to visit Shanghai would be honored and from there we lit out for the finance office where we changed our Indian money to American money.

After asking directions, we walked to the road where we dumped our bag and waited for a ride. Soon a jeep and trailer came along and we were headed for the city about 2 miles away. The first thing we noticed was the large number of whites (Europeans) that were working at the air base as chauffeurs, etc. In a few moments we learned that many of them were recent Jap internees. The jeep gave us a wild ride, and how he managed to avoid killing half a dozen Chinese is beyond me. They are everywhere. The roads are full of bicycles and bicycle cabs, and an American jeep is certainly a hazard — and there are plenty of them in Shanghai. It seems that from their markings every unit in the CBI must be stationed here.

We got to almost the center of town and tried to get a room in the Park Hotel. They were "full up!" No wonder — it seemed as tho ½ the Yank Navy stayed there. I pleaded with the room clerk, but to no avail. Finally he said that he'd direct us to another hotel which would put us up. He gave us a card, and wrote the address in both English and Chinese. With that card, he said we would get a place. Ha Ha - that Chinese was smart! For when we got to this hotel we found that they too were filled up. He got rid of us all right! But here the room clerk was an Austrian and after a lot of talking we convinced him that he ought to do something for us. He showed us the register. Living here were about 10 or 12 Generals, 5 Admirals and hundreds of Colonels. That convinced us — this place would be good enough! Finally we got a room. Here, I sit now. A large double room, as nice as any in the states, and better than most. Large and airy — really well furnished with bathroom, tub and shower etc. We've just been looking out of the window at Nanking Rd and there's a hell of a parade going on. Seems as tho this is just another one of those victory celebrations.

We are going to have dinner in the room tonite. I've just seen the menu and if the food is just 1/4 as good as it sounds — then this will be wonderful.

I've been thinking constantly of you Sweetest dearest Rosalind. Thinking that if only this month flies by - the next one may find me at the start of the long voyage home. I miss you so — want to be with you so!

While I'm here, I shall try to get some nice things for you. I want you to be happy, and I along with you.

Must run to the tub now! The first in such a long time. I shall sleep well tonite and dream of you dear and of our love. I adore you, dearest — sweetest Rosalind —

I love only you — I love you so!

CHICK

234

12 Oct. 45
Shanghai

Dearest, Sweetest, Adorable Ros,

The first day is over — and what a day. Burma and its sweat and grime is all but forgotten. How long has this place been in existence? Last nite we had a deliciously bountiful meal. Hold your hat and listen to this —

(1) Shrimp Cocktail
(2) Onion Soup
(3) Porter house steak
    French fried potatoes
    Mushrooms
(4) Salad, sliced tomatoes
(5) Baked Alaska (ice cream and cake covered
    by  meringue)
(6) Coffee —
Enough?

After that sumptuous repast there was nothing to do but sit around. Such rich food will certainly play hell with my gut. How I got all of that down, I don't know. If the rest of the food around town is near as good as this was, then I'll never eat at Myitkyina the way I did before. Always I thought "Well what the hell,  this is the best food around this neck of the woods." But after last nite and those meals today, I'll insist on their flying to Shanghai to get me food.

We sat around a while, and then put on our OD's (it was cool out) and decided to stroll about. As we left the Hotel, we were beset by Ricksha coolies who insisted that we ride. You've seen pictures of them, haven't you? There was no escape, so we rode. The streets were almost impass-able and everywhere there were soldiers and sailors and Europeans and Chinese. Noise there was aplenty and a staccato fire of Chinese fire-crackers. And pictures of Chiang Kai Shek? Millions of them. He must have a great publicity man. Now and then a shiny American car would creep by driven by a sleek looking Chinese. They are either really very rich here, or very, very poor. It seems that the streets are crowded with coolies. After an hour of this we made a detour to the Hotel and got ready for bed. We'd see the town in the AM. Time enough then.

This AM - I didn't want to get out of bed. Why should I? But I was hungry. So out I jumped into the shower. That must have awakened Marty for he got up too and after dressing at 9 AM we made our way to the dining room. What a breakfast!!

(1) American tomato juice
(2) Steak and 2 fried eggs.
(3) Toast, butter and Jam
(4) Milk and Coffee

Imagine having steak for Breakfast? We were raring to go now, but as we stepped into the lobby we ran into Ed Mayer and Dominick Quinn, two really swell guys from the 14th. They were looking for a room, too! Quick like our friend, the bunny — I up and had a heart to heart talk with our friend, the room clerk. Result — a small suite! A Colonel had just vacated. For $5.00 a day it was theirs. I came back with the key and thereupon they got down on their knees and delivered a short prayer to Allah Chaikin, the Miracle man. Of course, we had to wait for them now.

As we sat and waited, a fellow came over with a camera and asked if we wanted to buy one. He spoke with a German accent and I thought he must be Jewish. He was! We chatted fully 10 minutes and he told us about the Jewish Refugee Colony in Shanghai. We took his address and told him we'd accept his invitation to meet his wife. He recommended a restaurant which has really fine Russian food, "Constantinople." We made an appointment for tomorrow. The boys came down and now it was getting on. Time goes so fast in Shanghai. We decided to go to the Red Cross in Shanghai and we found them really well set up in a fine building with a soda fountain, et al.

While we changed American money into Chinese money, (1 American to 800 Chinese dollars), we ran into the two Majors and promptly invited them to dinner at the "suite." They are coming, due soon!

We rode out via Ricksha to the French Concession and there we found a number of nice shops operated by Jews, and I tried out my Yiddish and found it a highly successful enterprise. Soon I picked up a lot of local color from the neighborhood and it was lunch time.

To the Constantinople, and a wonderful meal

(1) Vodka
(2) Borscht (magnifique)
(3) Beef Stroganoff
(4) Podjarka
(5) More Vodka
(6) Coffee
(7) Champagne ($8.00 per bottle)

There were 6 of us, for we picked up two more GI's on the way (all of the 4th group must be goofing off here) and the food was beyond description. I wish I could write about it. I'll save it to tell you of it! There's so little I'd care to say about my stay overseas, that telling about Shanghai will be a pleasure. So we ate and drank and enjoyed ourselves immensely. My heart goes out to the poor bastards stationed here while awaiting shipment home. What a life!!

We rode to the Hotel quite happily and got here about 3:30. At 4, we were all napping. Dinner tonite is at 7:30 and now it's 6:45 and I have to wash up. More tomorrow, Darling.

Oh, Darling Ros. Someday, you and I will take a trip and vacation like this. This will be as nothing compared to the fine time we shall have. I love you so. The days fly by here. A couple of months, hardly longer than that. We'll be together then, with our love, I love only you.

CHICK

❖

When I read the first letter from Shanghai, I was furious. He had been writing steadily of the sorry condition of the C-46s, and given the choice of boat or plane for his return to the states, he chose the 28-day boat trip through the Suez canal to New York, saying he would not trust the "war weary" C-46s to make it back. Yet here he was, with nary a qualm, flying the treacherous Hump to Shanghai on a jaunt. Swept along in the wake of peace, he could not resist the opportunity to see Shanghai, Who could after so much boredom? It was a once-in-a-lifetime chance. But from where I was sitting, it was fraught with danger, and I was gripped with a stunning terror. Flying the hump was fair game for every kind of accident. It did not take too fanciful an imagination to feed the fearful thought of his plane going down, or a gun going off accidentally by some tipsy reveler, soldier, or sailor, in Shanghai. The whole 3rd group, part of the 4th, and what seemed like half the navy fleet were in town — all celebrating. To me it was a perfect scenario for a mishap. I suppose there was envy mixed with the fear. Shanghai, the most exotic city. I wanted to be there with Chick, I wanted to stay at the Cathay Hotel, see the sights, smell the smells, and share the adventure. Instead, here I was in the dull Bronx, doing the same mundane tasks. I was angry on all counts. His loving words did not help. I put aside my pen and stopped writing until he returned safely to his base in mid-October. It was better for him to find no letters waiting on his return than anything I would have written during those days.

Once back at the base, rumor and gossip was in full sway. He grappled with the endless boredom and unrestrained speculation about who was going home and when. With sixty-two points to his credit, he calculated he would leave India in December and arrive home the first part of January 1946. He was right. The first week of December he left for the port of embarkation, Karachi, and set sail for home on December 7th, 1945.

*In Shanghai*

*With Marty Gertler*

*Chick at ease*

*Riding via ricksha*

*Goodbye Burma Sky*

Chapter 19

## HE'S REALLY COMING HOME 1945-46

While Chick traveled the stormy December seas for 28 days and nights, I was busy setting up our apartment. I had saved the money from the sale of our car and now with the poker money in hand, I was able to furnish our little place.

It was a ground floor studio apartment with a view I chose to ignore — a back alley separating us from the apartment house next door. I was riveted instead on the indoor view — living/bedroom 12' by 14', bathroom, and full kitchen/dinette, all off a small foyer. From my point of view, a veritable palace!

My mother was as delighted as I. Not only was she thrilled on my account, but her life would be changing as well. The clutter in her apartment would vanish. Once again, she and my dad could luxuriate in their wide, springy bed as well as enjoy their living space with friends. Relaxed and happy, she outdid herself. We shopped together for furniture, linens and kitchen stuff. Often she chose to stay home with Robert — a treasured gift of valuable time for me to get things done. No matter the gray winter days, ours were bright and cheerful, filled with smiles.

Shipments were slow and I was eager to have everything in place before Chick arrived. I managed to arrange a fast delivery for an oval, natural wood, oak table and six padded chairs for the breakfast room. Since I expected we would entertain friends here in the evenings (while Robert slept in the big room), I wanted to brighten the area. I found a do-it-yourself wallpaper, shiny white with little roses scattered throughout, and papered the dinette wall panels. So charming, I thought then, (I wouldn't allow it out of the sample book today). With simple white curtains on the window, the kitchen-dinette was finished.

A wide, triple dresser was the perfect find to divide the large room. I gave Robert the far left side of the room where his bed, high-boy, bike, toy chest, games, and books created a private space for him. Our double bed would slide into the front corner of the room leaving plenty of open space when you entered. With a heavy textured throw and lots of colored pillows the bed could serve as a couch during the day. A radio, clock, and telephone completed the essentials.

Before deliveries, I waxed and polished the wood floors, and painted the raw wood dresser. Robert was excited by all the activity. His dad was coming home and he wanted to help. The amount of stuff this three-year-old could carry was startling. Little by little, after five and one-half years, our first home was coming together.

In the midst of these preparations I was thrilled to receive these letters from Chick aboard the U.S.S. General Brooke, something I never expected.

❖

13 December 1945
U.S.S. General Brooke

Dearest Sweetest Ros:

Strange, writing from aboard ship somewhere in the Indian Ocean. But our next scheduled stop is Port Said, near Suez and they tell me that a letter mailed there will get to NY before the boat docks.

Knowing how difficult mailless days are for you, I thought I'd get this one off, to break up that long siege of "no letter days."

This is the start of our sixth day at sea. Actually there should be only 21 sailing days left, and if we don't stop more than overnite to refuel etc. then the chances are good that we'll dock in N.Y. on the 3rd, even tho we're not officially due there until the 5th.

I have been extremely lucky ever since I left the 4th group. The first thing was to make this boat which left Calcutta early on the 8th. It was supposed to be the 3rd boat to leave this month, but actually it was the first! One boat left one day before us but we passed it in the Bay of Bengal. The second boat had just started loading when we pulled out of port.

You see, these sailing lists are made up days in advance, and if your boat is in, you load up. If it's not in, you wait. Our boat came in on time, loaded up and took off. The other two, for one reason or another, were late in coming and loading.

The sailors aboard say that the Capt. is anxious to make good time and that we ought to make it by the 3rd or 4th of Jan.

I have K.P every other nite from 6:30 to 1:00 AM. All our particular detail does is "eye" the potatoes. I've never seen so damn many spuds. There are about 4000 mouths to feed aboard and they really serve excellent meals. Three times a day. Yet in addition to this, we eat like pigs when we're on duty and if I don't stop that, I'll really put on weight. Sleeping accommodations are beastly — I won't even begin to describe them. But the boat is headed in the right direction and that makes up for everything. The trip has been rather smooth thus far and I feel swell. But it's so crowded darling, that every inch of deck space is utilized. Only the damned officers have swell cabins and lots of "promenade" space. We are surely "enlisted swine." But no matter. 30 days more, maybe less and I'll be thru with the whole lousy stinking setup.

When we dock, we go to Camp Shanks (near N.Y.) And we stay there from 24 to 48 hours. We can call and wire from there and you can bet I'll get thru to you even if it's 4 AM. Stick close to the house from the 2nd of Jan. on, and you won't miss the call.

Then we go to Fort Dix, N.J. where they say we wait from 3 to 5 days before we get on a separation roster. When we get on that list, it takes 48 hrs after that to get fully processed and out.

That period will be hell! That waiting. I'll size up the setup when I get to Dix and see if I can get a pass or steal out some way. If that's impossible, then visitors are allowed on the post. If only a car were available to you, it would be simple. Without one, the traveling is really quite hard. Traveling alone — perhaps it wouldn't be too bad. There are Penn Trains going to Ft. Dix etc. If you take an early one and leave on an evening train we can have a pleasant visit together.

Why don't you call Penn Station and get all the info? There are also buses that go there ( maybe even right to the camp). Then when I call from Dix and if I can't get a pass, I'll tell you where I'm located, at the base, and you can tell me when to expect you.

It would be simpler all around, if you had a car, to come alone. I don't know! Would you take Mom along?

Anyway, it surely is shaping up for us to be together in about 30 days or so. I hope that "separation" won't take as long as they say. *Life* magazine ran a story on it saying it only took 48 hrs. Another case of lying to those gullible civilians. Here aboard ship they told us 5 to 7 days to get out of Dix.

In about 2 days or so we should be at Port Said and this letter should be on its way to you.

At about that time, we should still have about 17 to 18 days of sailing. So when you're reading this, you'll do so with the knowledge that it "won't be long"

Sweetheart Dearest Ros! I love you so very much, with all my heart. All I think of is you and my blood races and my heart pounds so that I threaten to fall apart at the seams.

I do hope you've been having a pleasant time with the apartment. What a wonderfully gay time we'll have there. Once again to live that love we've been dreaming about during these long desolate months. Once again together, fully, completely, in every way.

That picture is constantly before me, and the happiness these thoughts bring can be exceeded only by the joy that the sight of you will bring.

I love you, Rosalind with every prayer, I hope that you and Rob are well and that we'll all be so happy — soon. I love only you.

CHICK

P.S. I now hear that we get to Port Said on the 20th of Dec. Then we should be in N.Y. about 14 or 15 days later. If this letter gets to you on the 2nd of Jan or before, you'll know that I'm only a few days from home.

Maybe I will be home for Wed, 9th Jan. If not I should certainly make it for Sat. the 12 Jan. We'll have a little party, just you, me and Robert.

I love you sweetest dearest Rosalind, with all my heart, I love you so!!

❖

I laughed when I read all the suggestions in his letter — call Penn station — get bus schedules — if you only had a car — come to camp, we could have a pleasant visit — he was losing it, I thought. The last thing I wanted, after fourteen months, was to see him for the first time at an army camp teeming with GI's. The very thought of it made me shudder. Then reality struck. He was really on his way! Up to this moment I had been going through the motions, getting ready, but now— I shivered with excitement, allowing myself to say for the first time, "He is really coming home — expect him any time now."

I tuned out all his suggestions, refusing to conjecture what the army would do. I decided kismet was in charge here. Then this last letter from the ship arrived.

❖

18 Dec. 45

Dearest Darling Ros

This is just about the eleventh day out of Calcutta and thus far everything seems to be going along quite well.

I think that the day after tomorrow will find us at Port Said, at the Mediterranean end of the Suez Canal. These letters are going to be mailed there and if the Naval Transport service is on the ball, you should get them before we dock.

We should leave Port Said on Dec. 21, and they say that it's 14 days from there to New York.

The trip tho really terribly boring, has in a boring manner, resolved itself into a somewhat pleasant undertaking. (Now what in hell does that mean)?

At any rate, I found a way of beating the racket. I worked up to now at KP peeling "eyes" out of the tons of spuds every other nite. I can quit that at Port Said, but I and a few others have decided to keep the detail but to take the day shift, that way, having a job to do makes the time go somewhat faster.

Then three others and myself have begun playing bridge and we have really swell games every day for several hours. We'll have to locate another couple who plays, darling, and maybe we'd do well to get hold of a "Book on Bridge" and both study up.

So with time for sleeping, washing, eating etc. the days do go by however slowly.

So often before I go to bed, my thoughts are completely of you, and the realization comes to me that I'm headed home and in about 24 days or less I will be completely out of the army. Home with you!! And I am then filled with such a yearning and longing and my heart pounds so that I feel that I must get up and run. I get so restless and I toss and turn and just lie awake and pictures of you flash thru my mind and I can't fall asleep but somehow I do, and with dawn comes another day.

By the time this gets to you, I may be on the Atlantic! We should dock on the 3rd or 4th. It will probably take 7 days to get out of the army. The chances of getting out before the 9th Jan are so slim. But I'll call and we'll see if we can see each other before I get out.

Only a little while longer, a few more steps. I love you so my darling. I adore you,

CHICK

❖

Not one of the rumors on army separation procedures was true. It all happened so quickly that Chick was released before he had time to formulate any plans at all. The lines at the telephones were a mile long; it was just simpler and smarter to get out and catch the train for New York City. Once he arrived in Penn Station, he quickly hopped the subway to the Bronx. Now, only minutes away from home, he stopped just long enough to phone me.

I was finishing some cleaning in the apartment, Robert was upstairs with my mother when his call came. Dressed in a messy housedress, my hair disheveled, I hardly had time to throw the cleaning rag down and run my fingers through my hair when the bell rang — and there he was. Eyes shining, that wide incandescent smile beaming across his face, joyous, exuberant — no more war, no more longing, no more anxiety. He was real, he had made it, and the time was now.

# *Epilogue*        1946-1991

*Karen, David, Eric, and Robert Chaikin*
*1954*

# EPILOGUE                                    1946-1991

The moment Chick and I walked into my parent's apartment on that memorable January day in 1946, Robert came flying down the foyer hall right into Chick's outstretched arms. He clung to Chick, bubbling and squealing with joy, as they hugged and kissed; Robert would not let go until Chick reached out to bring me into the circle of their embrace. I laughed and cried thinking my heart, so full, would burst. After so many months of separation and emptiness, I was alive again. A little tug of worry edged in, that fear of it being too good to be true, but I pushed it aside to savor every moment of sunshine.

The world lay ahead with boundless choices. Together, we could do anything — we'd raise a family, make friends, build a home, do our work and we were ready.

Soon after his home coming we moved to Springfield, Massachusetts, where Chick aggressively and successfully organized workers and made the union grow. He became a well-known presence in union activities, community life, and in politics throughout Western Mass. and other New England states. People who knew him said, "He was a firebrand, who ignited everyone and everything around him. His lust for life and learning was palpable."

As an outspoken Democrat in the city's political life, he was among the first supporters in his region of the young, up-and-coming John F. Kennedy, for Congress. In later years, he helped Kennedy receive the labor support he needed in his presidential race.

The forties and fifties were the baby-boom years, and New England was the happy place where our sons Eric and David, then daughter Karen were born. For me, Springfield is a synonym for ten wonderfully rich years. For Chick, these early years foreshadowed all his later accomplishments.

When Chick was promoted to Director of the Southwest Region in 1956, we moved to Dallas, Texas. His department included Oklahoma, Arkansas, Louisiana, and New Mexico, a vast territory, with few members. Anti-union sentiment prevailed there, and Chick found southwest employers more cold-spirited and less connected to their workers. In response, unions behaved like a movement under siege, huddling together for mutual aid and support.

These southwestern years were a broadening experience for us. It helped us see how varied the American people were. In San Antonio, we found the black haired, dark-eyed Mexicans, dressed in flamboyant colors, with temperaments to match, counterpoised against the sandy haired, blue-eyed sea of workers in Arkansas and Oklahoma. We heard the well organized, fundamentalist religious voices of some Christian sects, rigid and unyielding in their ultra conservative thought. We saw the undercurrent of hate when Christian children were forbidden, by their parents, to play with Catholic children on our street, and we met many people, black and white, eager for change. It helped us sort out a little better, the political differences within the country.

While Chick struggled with "right to work" laws, (which he dubbed, "right to work for less laws"), and worked at desegregating union meetings and factory lunch rooms, I took courses in Braille in order to transcribe books for blind children attending public schools. When I received my Library of Congress certification as a transcriber, it was time to move again, this time back to New York City in 1959.

We would miss the courtly and civil people, their famous hospitality, the twang of a Texas or southern drawl, and the musical rhythms of the mariachi, marimba and strumming guitars. Texas had been an adventure.

The move to New York opened the doors for his election as president of the ILGWU. In 1975 Chick became a national leader and international advocate for working people. No longer tethered to restrictive, negative surroundings, he was free to stretch his intellect and run with creative ideas. One, among many examples was the "Look For The Union Label" campaign he initiated in 1975. Chick was the first union leader to use television, radio, and bus ads to send his message across the country. He wanted the people, Congress and

252

the President to know who his workers were, that they worked hard and needed the jobs they were losing to unregulated imports. The song became a hit, and the message came across. People sing it even today.

Although organizing and negotiating for workers was always his primary task, he also understood that politics, the communities in which workers lived, and how their children were educated, were basic union concerns. He was active in all of it, enjoyed it thoroughly, and was good at it. With people, he shone.

Our children made new friends and adjusted to their new schools. I put my teaching credits together with my new Braille certificate and started teaching blind and visually handicapped children in the Nassau County public school system. It was the start of a nineteen year career during which I earned my master's degree, and began working with learning disabled children as well. As part of a team, where we helped teachers learn how to create individual programs for different children, I set up resource rooms in school districts around the county. I turned down offers to move up the career ladder, choosing instead to remain a teacher, which gave me the time for Chick and my family.

Chick also gave up things for his family. True to his word he resisted trips away from home. Though his work required that he travel, he would drive the roads, or take flights at very late hours to get home, often arriving at 3:00 or 4:00 in the morning. He refused most overnight stays, and when he could not say no to such an invitation he would urge me to join him. When we could not be together, he continued to write newsy, loving letters. Throughout the years, our private lives were intrinsically interwoven with his public life.

With each passing year, Chick became more widely known and regarded. He was often asked to business conferences or universities to present a paper, or to visit labor people in other lands. He would refuse these trips unless I could join him. I would hear him say on the phone, "Sorry, I can't do that, Ros can't go now, maybe another time." As a result we traveled only during my summer vacations in July and August.

After he became President of the ILGWU, (though Chick never asked), I retired in order to join him everywhere. My life became even more unusual and fulfilling

From the day of my retirement, Chick immediately began to accept more and more national and international invitations. He made it clear that his wife would accompany him wherever he traveled, and asked that I be invited to scheduled meetings and events. Much to the surprise of the American men, who insisted this would not play overseas, and certainly not in Asia, I was welcomed almost everywhere — in Thailand, Korea, even in Japan. The only exception was the Prime Minister of Japan who sent regrets; he did not permit women to attend his meetings. The places we went, the people we saw, opened worlds of diplomacy and international politics I could never have imagined.

As a vice-president of the AFL-CIO, Chick was the spokesman on many Solidarity Team visits. The purpose was to extend a hand of friendship to beleaguered trade unions outside the US, listen to the workers, and always speak for a democratic solution to their problems in his interviews even with the most autocratic government officials.

And so, I was there in 1977, in Brazil, an emerging nation, where rates of pay and raises were controlled by the state; where there was no collective bargaining and no right to strike. We saw Rio de Janeiro, the "soul" of the country, "fun city" where ocean and living went together, where beaches and Samba ruled. Its abject poverty lay undisguised alongside excessive wealth, in a city, nestled between mountains and sea.

We saw the "heart" of the country, Sao Paulo, an industrial city, where we visited metal workers, telephone workers, communication workers, and ended the day at a small night club called Stardust. The owner, a Jew, born in Germany, had fled across Manchuria to Shanghai, to Israel and on to Brazil. He was a sensational piano player who looked so much like Hoagy Carmichael that we began to think we must be in "Casablanca" as part of some fantasy film. For the first hour he played all the tunes of the 1940's for our dancing pleasure.

We flew to Brazilia, where Rio people said only the insensitive could live. "A place with no soul," they said, "a kind of Siberia." In 1977, it was a pioneer town, a city just begun, new and modern, so much sameness. There we met the MAN. He walked out of the written pages of history and came alive for us, Ary Campista, president of the National Confederation of Industrial Workers (CNTI). He was heartily disliked by many free trade unionists for "collaborative tactics;" an exciting personality, reaching out for better US/Brazil relationships.

I was there in Buenos Aires, Argentina, on a human rights issue, where labor people, among others, were being kidnapped and tortured; where the Madres of the Plaza were marching, demanding to know where their loved ones were. When the mothers heard that the wife of the leader had accompanied him on this trip, they asked to come up to see me. A few came up to thank me for having made this long exhausting trip. They said it was very important to them to know that their message was getting out to other women, and asked if we would plead their cause.

I watched Chick confront the triumvirate of beribboned Generals in full uniform, before speaking to the Labor minister, where he asked for the release of a list of people. Shortly after we arrived home, he was notified that some people listed were found and released.

I was there in 1978, in Chile, where Chick led a delegation of five at a meeting with President Augusto Pinochet, the military dictator of Chile. He had come to present the case that a free trade union movement was the best defense against the communist threat that Pinochet feared. It was an extraordinary conversation that lasted two hours, after which Chick presented a list of men who had been imprisoned, and asked for their release. Here too, he was successful—most of the men on the list were released.

I was there in Egypt, right after Sadat's visit to Jerusalem in 1978, when George Meany asked Chick to meet with Egyptian labor people, to encourage them in their direct peace negotiations with Israel.

I was there in Tokyo at the Labor Summit in 1979 (but not permitted to see the Prime Minister), when Chick pleaded in defense of the Indo-Chinese refugees.

I was there in South Africa in 1982, to meet with leaders of the newly emerging black unions. It was the first time the South African apartheid government permitted an AFL-CIO group to enter the country.

I was there at the White House, on many occasions, to meet with President and Mrs. Jimmy Carter, including a private lunch in their living quarters. And I was there when Chick seconded the nomination of President Carter in 1980.

I was there at meetings with workers, business groups, government members and academicians, in the US and around the world, too numerous to mention.

The trips, the adventures, what were they for me? Wives often travel with their husbands. Traditionally they shop, sight see, and attend garden parties while the men work. Although these activities are both enjoyable and educational, they learn second hand about the events taking place. Chick made me a participant in his work. I was an eye witness, learning first hand, about people, government practices, freedom and oppression.

Over the years we both enjoyed exceptionally good health until February of 1983, when Chick suffered a heart attack. A series of tests revealed considerable heart damage. The news sickened and terrified me, but Chick simply moved past it and looked ahead. Within a few weeks, medication made it possible for him to go back to work full time, with very few changes in his schedule.

Seven years later, retired from the ILGWU, and now CEO of the Jacob Javits Convention Center he underwent emergency surgery to by-pass several large abdominal aneurysms in the aorta — a surgery that further weakened his heart but not his optimistic outlook.

On his birthday in January 1991, we were getting ready to go out and celebrate. I glanced over, and caught sight of him combing his hair, still thick and wavy, shining silver in the light. He was dressed in an elegant black silk suit, white shirt, and beautifully patterned tie, and his new slim figure made him look younger and more handsome than ever to me. I walked up close and said, "Chick you really look great!"

He laughed and said, "Well, I made it Ros, seventy-three years."

"You'll make seventy-five too," I added.

Smiling that small smile I knew so well, he wrinkled his nose, shook his head slowly from side to side and said, "Seventy-five? No, I don't think so." Then, placing his hands on his abdomen where his surgical scars lay, he said, "It's not right, it's just not right."

I was shaken by his comment. In my own thoughts about his health, I recognized that Chick would probably not have a long life, but this last comment told me that much more than his heart was "not right." None-the-less, I felt certain he had several years ahead; there was so much life in him that I could still see. I said, "Yes, you will; you'll make seventy-five."

The months that followed were delightful. He was fully retired, thoroughly enjoying the relaxation and absence of any schedule. He slept late, read the newspapers, and made plans to raise funds for the Heller School at Brandeis University. We enjoyed our time together, looked forward to movies and theater, visited friends and they us. I'd hear him say to everyone he'd meet, "I've had the best life, I have no regrets." Each time, I'd wonder, "Is he sending us all a message?"

In March, the medication he had been taking began working against him, and the ominous symptoms of heart failure appeared. On occasion he would have trouble sleeping through the night.

On Sunday, March 31, 1991, Chick awakened rested from a deep and healing sleep that was a luxury those last two weeks. Refreshed, he showered, shaved, and dressed. I thought, "His body is adjusting." Friends dropped by all day. He laughed and talked about politics, about the dangerous world in which we lived, about what the real pleasures of life were. He said, "Family and a good night's sleep are at the top of that list."

Sunday night he could not get comfortable. I did not hear him slip quietly out of bed and tip-toe down the stairs to wait for morning. I found him sitting in his favorite chair in the den trying to soothe a wildly pulsating heart.

"Why didn't you call me?" I asked.

"I cannot do this any more," he said, quietly stroking his chest.

Frightened at the sight of his heart beating so violently, as though it would surely jump out of his body, I quickly rushed to help him into warm clothes, socks and slippers in order to get him to the hospital. Strangely the activity calmed the heart beat, and his breathing became more normal. Just then our son David arrived, seemingly heaven-sent.

We had forgotten that yesterday he had agreed to drive Chick to an early morning meeting in the city. Instead, David had arrived in perfect time to take us to the hospital. It was April 1, 1991. Once Chick was breathing easily and help was at hand, I told David he could leave and come back later in the day.

Waiting to be taken to a room, Chick was sitting in a wheel chair for the first time. Before the doctors, nurses, or interns descended upon us, I snatched the moment to kiss him gently and say, "I love you Chick." He held my hand and spoke the words he'd written over and over, and said afterwards so many times to me, "Ros, I've loved you so much , so much." I did not know it was good-bye. We had no other moment.

All the promises and longings, the wishes and yearnings he had written of, in the letters and poems turned out not to be empty fantasies of a lonely soldier. Chick was dreaming of a life's partnership. That's what we had. Over the years, we fashioned a life anchored to each other, with a lead long enough to move freely, strong enough to know its pull. All this together with a growing family of children and grandchildren to love.

We were given fifty-one unconstrained, exceptional and passionate years together.

*Chick and Ros 1976*

*Chick and Ros 1982*

THE CHAIKIN FAMILY 1991
Seth, Kim, Robert, David, Eric, Kyle, Allison, Shari, Chick, Lee
Nikki, Marilyn, Stacey, Shana, Rebecca, Rosalind, Karen, Zachary
Greg, Reed

# *Remembrances*

*He was a wonderful friend. He was there when you needed him, ready to educate, to help, to try to make things better in the big and in the little aspects of life. He didn't passively accept wrongs. He fought to make them right.*

Judge Jack B. Weinstein, friend

*Passion is the word that describes Chick. But mostly where it concerned people - in poverty, health, how they lived. He had so many interests. Articulate - oh I know lots of articulate people-but Chick was in a separate category. He came at things in a global way - an international view. He was unusual.*

Professor Stuart Altman, the Heller School of Social Welfare

*...The first thing Chick Chaikin ever asked of me was that I run for the United States Senate, and I would not have done it if he hadn't....and in between there were many other requests. He never asked anything for himself. It was always for others, and not those you would necessarily expect.*

Senator Daniel Patrick Moynihan

*Whenever I needed help as President, Chick was there. He embodied the best in American values. He was tough but compassionate. He set a shining example of a commitment to the brotherhood of all men and women, a commitment to human rights, a fervent dedication to just causes which will long leave an imprint on our nation.*

Jimmy Carter

*Chick was proud of his Jewish religious heritage, loved its beautiful traditions and helped many of its important institutions—from Brandeis University and Long Island Jewish Medical Center, to the American Ort Federation.... he was a key link between the American labor movement and Israel's Histadrut. Chick also carried Judaism's commitment to social justice and compassion into the public arena of American life. No one was a more articulate advocate for the right of working people to live in dignity and of the disadvantaged to enter the rich mainstream of American life.*

Stuart Eizenstat, friend

*If you want one word, I'd say exciting. He was an exciting man. There was nothing static about him. Intelligent, active — I think of the Sunday afternoon discussions we had. He argued forcefully and knew how to make his points — but never defended a position past a logical counter argument. He would come around if you could make him see your point. He had an agile mind, was passionate about everything he did, never passive or indecisive, a leader.*

Phyllis Barell, friend

*He was a leader — dynamic, intelligent. People came to him for advice and help — emotional, practical, political. I went to him for financial advice. No matter how busy he was, he made himself available. When we sat and talked, he knew the right questions to ask. I never felt hurried. He listened carefully, understood just what I was looking for. He pointed out the pitfalls, how to avoid them, and explained my options. Once I understood my choices better, I could make decisions. He then outlined how I might go about it, and always left the door open. The things he helped me with will carry me to the twenty-first century.*

Delia Gottlieb, friend

*Charming, he could charm anyone at all. Forceful. He took command of a group — became the center — had a reservoir of knowledge on almost any topic and aroused in you the need to disagree - we argued a lot and I loved it.*

Rae Webber, friend

*If he respected you he was patient, listened, and would give you time. If he didn't respect you he would simply walk away. I was constantly amazed at his fund of knowledge and his ability to recall the details on any subject. He encouraged me to leave the job where I was unhappy — helped me get a different start — he changed my life.*

Mal Webber, friend

*He was straightforward — no airs. I saw him at meetings and conferences. He listened a lot, his head cocked, sometimes a wry smile would appear — his face was never passive, it always reflected some emotion. He never stole the stage from anyone else. When he spoke, he always had something important to say — with humor and good sense.*

Betty Heller, board member, Family and Children's Policy
Center at the Heller School of Social Welfare

*I did't know him in his working life. I saw him when we had dinner, the four of us, now and again. But you and I were friends Ros, and what I remember most were the occasions I was in your house when he arrived home from work. He had a very expressive face. Each time, when he crossed the threshold and saw your face, it was like he was seeing you for the first time. His face would change and take on an expression of pure joy. He was totally connected to you.*

Ruth Englander, friend

*The first thing I think about is how deeply he loved my mother. No one could doubt that she was the center of his universe. The letters and poems he sent her during World War II expressed his feelings then; his actions during my lifetime only confirmed the depth of his feelings during their 53 years together.*

Robert E. Chaikin

*He considered himself a lucky man. He lived a life that exceeded his wildest dreams and had absolutely no regrets. He had gone on a journey and taken his family with him. He was a trace. We remember his light-hearted spirit and humor, his sense of purpose and immense intellect. He is in many respects a legend in his own time.*

Eric B. Chaikin

*Dad was tough, always fighting for working men and women here and abroad. He never wavered from fighting the good and just fight. I have regrets about our relationship. The most painful is that he died too soon — our souls were beginning to talk. I miss him deeply.*

Daivd R. Chaikin

*He was generous of spirit. I never knew anyone so generous, so giving — always there with an inclination to help.*

Karen Chaikin

## HIS HAIR WAS BLACK

*Lustrous in the light*
*glistening in the sun*
*wavy like a rippling bay.*
*Caught in the rain*
*it would curl ringlets round his head.*
*He would not permit that*
*and like the movie character*
*who whipped out a comb to puff-up his pompadour*
*he too carried a comb*
*using it now and again to tame the waves.*
*His children, tickled at the gesture*
*shook their heads in disbelief.*

*She came to know the supple feel of his hair*
*finely-textured*
*a thick downy softness against her skin*
*growing gentler with age*
*as gray strands brought new glints*
*to soften his face*
*slipping easily into silver*
*becoming the touch of silk.*

Rosalind B. Chaikin

## *SOMETHING SO DEEP INSIDE IS BROKEN*

*They ask her children, "How is mother?"*
*Her children say, "She is doing well*
*we all miss Dad so much*
*yes, she is fine, she goes everywhere*
*enjoys her friends, keeps busy*
*it's even hard sometimes to make a date with her."*

*In the quiet hours at home alone*
*she feels his irrepressible spirit*
*in and among their collected treasures.*
*She sees him sitting on the edge of their bed*
   *brushing his shoes to a high gloss each morning*
   *before his shower.*
*Knotting his tie in a perfect double Windsor*
   *the colors coordinated with his suit and socks.*
*The times she picks him up after work*
   *men exiting the building are tired,*
   *jackets off, ties askew.*
*He emerges fresh as the morning*
   *suit unruffled, tie in place, shoes still gleaming.*

*Reading in the evenings looking up*
   *she sees him gazing at her tenderly.*
*A smile begins as their eyes meet*
*And sometimes*
   *his strong hands with those long elegant fingers*
   *reach out to stroke her gently.*

*In a parade of memories she recalls how*
*  he reassured her, ruffled her,*
*     calmed, crazed and cradled*
*       teased and comforted*
*         angered and distressed her.*

*When he said, "You are my life"*
*His words  meant in love*
*     filled her with fear and trembling*
*knowing the days without him would come*
*Not knowing what she would do when*
*     Something so deep inside is broken.*

Rosalind B. Chaikin

Seconding the nomination of Jimmy Carter, 1980.

*Photo by Burton Berinsky*

# *Biography*

## SOL CHICK CHAIKIN                    1918-1991

B orn in New York City on January 9, 1918, Sol Chick Chaikin was the only one of Sam and Beckie Chaikin's three children to live past childhood. His parents, Russian Jews who had immigrated to the United States on or about 1910, worked in the garment industry, and were active members of the ILGWU. The Chaikins lived for a while in Harlem and Brooklyn before settling in the Bronx. At an early age he acquired the nickname Chick which he later adopted as a middle name. After attending public elementary school he was accepted at Townsend Harris Hall High School for academically gifted young men where students completed a rigorous 4 year course of study in 3 years. When he graduated in 1934 at age 16, he was class president and valedictorian; president of the history club, delegate to the school's General Organization (G.O.), business manager for his year book, Crimson & Gold, dubbed The Rising Sol and voted most capable.

Chick entered The City College of New York (CCNY), was elected president of his class, and became an eager supporter of the House Plan, an organization in formation at the time. In lieu of fraternities, the House Plan promised, a place where socially and culturally hungry urban college youth could associate together, and also meet with faculty outside the classroom. He became a leader in the group of enterprising young freshmen who set about building active House sections and raising funds from prominent alumni to purchase a 10 room brownstone at 292 Convent Ave. The building stands today as does a thriving House Plan. In 1938 he was managing director of the class book, Microcosm. His college vita reads: Solomon Chaikin, BSS Major Insignia; Vice Chancellor, Lock and Key; President, House Plan Council, Sim '38; Class President; Student Council; Chairman, Junior Prom Committee.

In June 1940, Chick graduated from Brooklyn Law School with an LL.B degree cum laude. In August 1940, he passed the New York State bar exam, was hired by President David Dubinsky as an organizer with the International Ladies' Garment Workers' Union (ILGWU) and married Rosalind Bryon.

The 1930's had been a time of great expansion and promise for American labor unions. Highlighted by the passage of the National Labor Relations Act, the Fair Labor Standards Act, and the formation of the C.I.O. Caught up in the fervor of the burgeoning labor movement, Chaikin decided he was more interested in working for the ILGWU than in a career as a lawyer.

From 1940 to 1943 he was assigned to New England. After organizing in Fall River and Boston for a few months he took on the job of business agent in Lowell, Massachusetts.

On July 30, 1943 he was inducted into the U.S. Army. His three-year World War II Air Force Service included 14 months with the Allied Air Corp. Combat Cargo Task Force in the China Burma India theater. Discharged with the rank of Sergeant in January 1946, he returned to New England to manage ILGWU Local 226 in Springfield, Massachusetts.

The Springfield area included all of the northeast states — north to Maine and south to Connecticut. Free from army service, at 28 Chaikin brought all his pent-up energy and intellect to his work. For ten years he aggressively and successfully organized workers throughout the state and region, while also accepting other responsibilities. He raised money for the Wesson Memorial Hospital, YMCA, United Fund, the Springfield Symphony, and for the fledgling Brandeis University. He worked with the Dunbar Community League advocating for the civil rights of the black community. He offered a human view to business leaders, civic clubs (Rotary, Kiwanis, women's groups, etc.), and college students on a wide range of topics. At Amherst, Mt. Holyoke, and Smith he lectured on labor issues including the intricacies of collective bargaining, why a union shop matters, organizing techniques and the fears of working people, their vulnerability and the protection unions offered. At the University of Massachusetts, he discussed the Connecticut River Development Project. Invited by bankers he titled his address "Why I Hate Bankers" starting humorously with an Ogden Nash poem — *Bankers live in marble halls because they encourage deposits and discourage withdrawals* — and then proceeded to charm them with his clear understanding of banking practices and problems, and their effect on working people.

Chick became a political force in the Springfield Democratic Party, and led organized labor unions to actively support and raise funds for the then Governor, Paul A. Dever; Jack Kennedy in his run for the House and then Senate, Foster Furcolo for the House, Senate and later for Governor of the state. In May 1954 he organized the first public meeting in Springfield against Senator Joseph McCarthy whose intimidating attacks on basic American freedoms had silenced so many others. With the Senator from Oregon, Wayne Morse (who changed party affiliation from a Republican to Democrat that year), as the lead speaker, people filled the auditorium to listen, and show their opposition to McCarthy.

Chick's union work never faltered. Recognized as a skillful organizer and negotiator, he could obtain major concessions from employers even when bargaining from a weak position.

Chick was asked to take on the directorship of the Lower Southwest Region and in 1956 moved with his wife and four children, to Dallas, Texas. The Southwest Region included Texas, Arkansas, Oklahoma, Louisiana and New Mexico. This huge territory with few garment workers and slim opportunities to organize, was essentially hostile to unions and hardly a stone's throw from the tar and feathering days. Running a union organizer out on-a-rail-was common place. It was a difficult uphill fight for Chaikin who believed strongly that a society is judged by what those who have the most, do for those who have the least. Here he found many who had so much, but were geared to give the least.

In 1959 he was recalled to the national headquarters to serve as Assistant Director of the Northeast Department, the largest single unit in the ILGWU that included New York, New Jersey, Pennsylvania, along with the New England states.

In the years 1959 - 1975 the flood of apparel into this country from almost no-wage countries of the Third World presented an ever increasing threat to the United States garment industry and workers' jobs. Chick reached out to other unions, business interests, legislators and academicians. He fought to create a dialogue among labor, business and government to help develop an international trade policy that would allow for imports, but at the same time not impoverish American workers. In his speeches he addressed the massive movement of capital, factories, technology and managerial skills by multinational corporations to other lands with no concomitant investment in U.S. industry. He understood the game of "transfer pricing" with which multinationals could end up paying little or no taxes on the multi-millions they earned — understandably an irresistible incentive to invest overseas.

During these years, membership of the ILGWU was changing. In the early formative years members were mainly Jewish and Italian males. By the 1970's almost 80% were women in a mix of white, black, Hispanic, and Asian. Different cultures and varied languages, made them more vulnerable. The garment factory was historically an entry level job they could not afford to lose. Without language and extensive training, they could easily be dumped on the welfare rolls. Furthermore, American consumers were not benefiting fully from the cheap labor that produced garments overseas. Apparel was purchased at low prices abroad, which were then jacked up to whatever the "traffic would bear." Chick concluded there could be no remedy to the import problem without some level of legislation and regulation.

Chick worked to elect Congress-people and Governors in each state in his region who he hoped would support his working members, In 1960 he felt that ILGWU President Dubinsky should meet with John F. Kennedy. Dubinsky had been backing Adlai Stevenson for President in the Democratic party primaries. He was not impressed with Kennedy's record in Congress, but he agreed to accept a phone call. Chaikin arranged for Robert Kennedy to call first. When Dubinsky picked up the call he heard, "President Dubinsky, this is Jack Kennedy's business agent." Dubinsky's laughter signaled that the ice had been broken — he loved it!

Within the Union, Chaikin struggled with inefficient practices, an outmoded piece-rate payment system, dated investment policies as employers confronted higher production costs, and imports continued to flood the country. He offered on-going training programs to staff, used industrial engineers to assess efficiency in the workplace, and involved employers in the effort to train and restructure.

In 1965 he was elected an ILGWU Vice President, and in 1973 General Secretary Treasurer under President Louis Stulberg who had succeeded Dubinsky in 1966. In 1975, he was elected President of the ILGWU, a Vice President of the AFL-CIO and a member of the Executive Council.

## THE CHAIKIN PRESIDENCY

When Chick was elected president of the ILGWU in 1975, the country was just coming out of the deepest recession since 1929. The union's very existence was threatened because of the impact of imports. The bleak prospects were made more difficult because the political pendulum had swung to economic conservatism. The 1970's were the Republican Nixon and Ford years and even the Democratic Carter years continued the conservative trend. With the Reagan administration, the pendulum swung further to the right. Unemployment grew with each recession. By 1985 a jobless rate of 7%, that was called a "recession" under Carter, was termed a "recovery" under Reagan. Between 1972 and 1984 almost 2 1/2 million manufacturing jobs had been lost; in apparel and textile industries more than 675,000 jobs were lost.

Despite these unfavorable developments, under Chaikin's leadership, the ILGWU continued to play a creative role in the industry, in the economy, in domestic political battles, and in the struggle for human rights internationally. Sol Chick Chaikin came to be known nationwide and worldwide. An outline of his years in office follows.

## THE GARMENT INDUSTRY AND THE UNION

### IMPORTS

1975... Chaikin initiated the ground-breaking "Union Label" campaign featuring the "Look for the Union Label" song with ILGWU workers and choir making their statement. The union sought name recognition and hoped to create a sympathetic climate across the country for union workers trying to "make it in the USA." It also spoke to business, government and all workers, organized and unorganized. While the TV messages worked their way into the minds and hearts across the country, Chaikin helped to create **The Fiber, Fabric Apparel Coalition for Trade** (FFACT), an affiliation of high level garment and textile employers who joined with the ILGWU and related unions to lobby in Washington.

1975-1985... Chaikin was an active lobbyist, engaged in solo or group meetings with legislators or giving congressional testimony; he was a public advocate, appearing on numerous national radio and TV shows, debates, and discussions, and was a pivotal force in the activities of FFACT.

1984... He started the legislative process rolling with a Sense of the Congress Resolution which called upon the Administration to roll back imports. It passed both houses handily.

1985... Senator Ernest F. Hollings of South Carolina and Representative Ed Jenkins of Georgia became the primary sponsors of the Textile and Apparel Trade Enforcement Act, designed to tie the rate of increase in imports to the growth in domestic consumption. The bill won overwhelming support in both houses of Congress but was vetoed by President Reagan. The vote to override the veto which required a two-thirds vote in each house of the Congress lost by 2 votes. The effort to slow down the onslaught of imports was lost.

MINIMUM WAGE...Chaikin led the effort to create a rational ratio between the legal minimum and the average wage in manufacturing. A compromise was enacted into law in the form of higher

minimums to go into effect in successive stages. It became part of the Fair Labor Standards Act.
STANDARDIZED and improved national industry agreements.
IMPROVED investment policy. Brought in professionals to invest the Union's monies and incorporated the Sullivan principles that barred investment in countries that abused human rights.
IMPROVED retirement pensions 12.5%. Reduced unfunded liability of the national retirement fund.
INITIATED alcoholism project at union health center.
STAFF TRAINING...Instituted leadership training for women and minorities - organizer training - Health and Safety training. Chaikin himself gave a productivity seminar for more than 200 industry executives.
OTHER ISSUES...Sweatshops - homework - industrial policy - enterprise zones - the Caribbean Basin Initiative - Immigration policy - item 807 of the U.S. Tariff Codes.

## POLITICS

Senator Daniel Patrick Moynihan has said, " ...*the first thing Chick Chaikin ever asked of me was that I run for the United States Senate, and I would not have done it if he hadn't.*" Chaikin spear headed the labor drive to elect Edward Koch as mayor of New York City and Mario Cuomo as governor of New York state. He urged the AFL-CIO to support Pat Moynihan for the U.S. Senate.
1976...As delegate to the Democratic National Convention, he supported and campaigned for Jimmy Carter for President.
1977...Attended Jimmy Carter's inauguration.
1979...Spoke at first dinner announcing President Carter's campaign for re-election.
1979...Present at signing of Israel-Egypt Peace Treaty at White House.
1980...Seconded President Carter's nomination for re-election, the first and only labor person so honored.
1983...Only labor leader in Democratic Party's formal response to "State of the Union" address.
1984...Early supporter of Walter Mondale for President.

1976, 1980, 1984...Organized garment center rallies for Democratic Party nominees .

## INTERNATIONAL REPRESENTATION

1976...International Textile, Garment, and Leather Workers Federation, (ITGLWF) Dublin Conference

1978...ITGLWF Tel Aviv Conference

1978...Chief fraternal delegate at German Clothing and Textile Workers' Union

1979...Addressed National Union of Tailors and Garment Workers, England.

1977...As the AFL-CIO representative to the International Labor Summit in London he engaged in a dialogue with Prime Minister James Callaghan.

1978...December- Member U.S. delegation at the funeral of Golda Meir, Israeli leader and former Israeli Prime Minister. She knew him as a friend from his days as the National Chairman of the Trade Union Council for Histadrut,(the Israeli labor federation), 1968-1973.

1979...Labor representative to International Labor Summit in Japan. He limited his remarks to energy and labor standards, stressing the need for a coordinated plan to negotiate price and distribution of supplies with the major OPEC oil-producing countries. He also suggested an approach to promote international labor policy that would raise low pay rates in all countries and promote better living standards.

June 22, 1979...Following the close of the Labor Summit Chaikin sought and received an audience with Prime Minister Masayoshi Ohiro as the representative of the AFL-CIO in order to plead for the rescue of many more Indo-Chinese refugees.

1980...U.S. worker delegate at International Labor Organization (ILO) session in Geneva.

1980...Addressed Histadrut in Israel.

1981...Chief fraternal delegate at British Trade Union Congress, (TUC) Conference.

1982…Delegate at International Confederation of Free Trade Unions, (ICFTU) session in Brussels the first time the AFL-CIO participated since 1968.

1982…Met in Japan with regional (Southeast Asia) reps of garment and textile workers' unions.

1985…Hosted Zensen (Japanese sister union) delegation at session in New York.

ACADEMICS AND HUMAN RIGHTS

Membership/trustee in pro-human rights organizations: Amnesty International, International Rescue Committee (IRC), Freedom House.

**Delegate to Helsinki Accords Conferences** officially known as the Commission for Security and Cooperation in Europe (CSCE) - Belgrade in 1977 and Madrid in 1980. In his speech entitled *The Solidarity of US Labor Swung Open the Doors of My prison Cell*, Vladimir Bukovsky said, "Only one voice spoke out in defense of human rights — Chick Chaikin, president of the International Ladies' Garment Workers' Union and your representative at the Belgrade Conference.

Member of the Workers' Commission of the International Sakarhov Hearings.

Chaired a special committee of the Economic Policy Council of the United Nations Association.

Commission of US Brazil Relations.

**Membership in International Affairs Organizations** —

Trilateral Commission — by its own description, a "private North American, West European, Japanese initiative on matters of common concern." Its membership included academicians, management representatives, labor leaders, financial experts, members of Congress and others from western industrialized nations, including Japan.

Council on Foreign Relations.

Atlantic Council of the United States.

National Committee for Labor Israel.

International advocacy of human rights/trade union rights.

1976...Spoke at bicentennial salute to captive nations at Battery Park/Statue of Liberty.

1976... In June, following the death of Spain's fascist dictator Francisco Franco, Chaikin met with Amadeus Cuito of Catalonia, and Antonio Garcia Lopez and Luis Madriaga Solana in Madrid. These trade union leaders in the social democratic movement were seeking to create a free society in Spain, and looking to open up lines of communication with the world, in particular with the US labor movement.

1977...Meeting with trade unionists in Brazil.

1977...Meeting with Argentine junta to seek release of jailed human rights and trade union activists.

1978...Meeting in Egypt with trade unionists to encourage detente with Israel.

1978...Two hour meeting with General Pinochet, dictator of Chile to seek restoration of free trade unions, human rights, and the release of imprisoned labor leaders.

1978...Coordinated boycott by North and South American trade unions of Chile, Cuba, and Nicaragua to protest repressive regimes.

1979...Representative at International Sakharov Hearings.

1979...Meeting with newly formed General Workers Union (UGT), in Portugal, and with leaders of the New Socialist Party.

1979...Argentina - protest the unjustified arrest of 20 trade unionists.

1982...Led first official delegation to meet with newly emerging black trade unions in South Africa.

OTHER INTERNATIONAL APPEARANCES

1976...Paris World Organization for Rehabilitation Training (ORT) Conference.

1978...Asian American Free Labor Institute (AAFLI) trip to Southeast Asia.

1978...Dedicated Luigi Antonini Library at University of Catania, Italy.

1978...Addressed Ministers of Labor from North and South America in Peru.

1980...Addressed International Chamber of Commerce in Brussels on "Trade and Employment in the Textile and Apparel Industries: An Industrialized Country View."

1984...Dedicated Louis Stulberg Hospital in Israel.

1985...Invited to speak with **Keidanren**, the Japanese equivalent of the National Association of Manufacturers, the leading economic force in the country. Told that Chaikin was among the most knowledgeable, they wished to discuss the American labor movement with him along with Japanese management systems. They were planning to increase their automobile divisions in the U.S. and looking to better understand American labor systems.

1985...American European Community Association to the Hague on American Labor Movement.

## COLLEGE AND UNIVERSITY ADDRESSES

1979...In keynote address, called on American Council on Education to join with Labor movement to study issues of mutual concern..

1980...Featured speaker at Stanford University at the first national symposium on the status of Soviet and Eastern Block dissidents.

1980...Began regular lectures to Presidential Classroom for Young Americans, Harvard Business School, Northwestern Business School, Columbia University Arden House program.

1982... Commencement address at Rutgers University.

1983...Organizing committee for First National Conference on Science and Labor.

1983...AFL-CIO Rights Conference.

1983...Led seminar at Yale University Southern African Research Program.

1984...Resource person for U.S. Bishops Conference on the American Economy, Notre Dame University.

1985...Addressed Eastern Educational Consortium on novel approaches to adult education.

1986...Addressed Foreign Service Institute
Lecture at Martin Luther King Jr. Center for non-violent social change.

PUBLISHED WORKS: Book, Articles, Speeches

1980...*A Labor Viewpoint : ANOTHER OPINION*, Foreword by Daniel P. Moynihan, (Library Research Associates Inc.)

1980...Journal of Socioeconomic Studies , *"Labor's Critical Issue, the Two-Tiered Society."*

1982...Foreign Affairs *"Trade, Investment and De-Industrialization: Myth and Reality."*:

1983...International Development Conference, *"Towards a Rational Development Policy."*

1984...*"The Politics of Industrial Policy,"* compendium.

1985...Touche-Ross compendium on trade. 1986 Democratic policy commission.

1985...National Coordinating Committee for Multi-employer Plans (NCCMP), *"A Look at Health Care."* Suggested ways to set up new systems for delivering health care in a more cost effective manner.

## CIVIC AND SOCIAL POLICY SERVICE ORGANIZATIONS

The American Veteran's Committee, The Jewish Labor Committee, The Workmen's Circle

1969...Trustee of the Long Island Jewish/Hillside Medical Center

1974-86...Board of Directors New York Urban Coalition

1976-86...Member of Board of Directors of the Urban League and National Association for the Advancement of Colored People (NAACP)

1982...Member Governor's special Transit Advisory Panel. New York City Water Conservation Board.

1982...Appointed to the board of Jacob Javits Convention Center (JJCC) Operating Corporation.

Elected Chairman of the JJCC Operating Corp. (date uncertain)

1985...Ford Foundation Executive Panel on Social Welfare, that published in May 1989, a framework for a national discussion entitled "The Common Good: Social Welfare and the American Future."

## ACADEMIC AFFILIATIONS

1979...Trustee of Brandeis University
Trustee of the Fashion Institute of Technology (FIT).
1983...Established the Rosalind and Sol Chick Chaikin Institute of Hematology —Oncology at the Long Island Jewish/Hillside Medical Center, Schneider Children's Hospital.
1983...Dedication of Sol C. Chaikin Chair in National Health Policy at the Florence Heller Graduate School for Advanced Study in Social Welfare, Brandeis Unviersity.
1986...Member of Board of Overseers, The Heller School.
1989...Elected Chairman of the Board of Overseers, The Heller School.
1978...Townsend Harris Medal for Notable Achievement and placed in its Hall of Fame.
1980...Honorary Doctor of Humane Letters degree at Rutgers University.
1980...Honorary Doctor of Humane Letters degree at City University of New York (CUNY).
1986, June...At 68, Chick retired as ILGWU president. Still active, he became a member of the Bd of Directors of the Custodial Trust Co. and continued his affiliations with JJCC, Brandeis University, the Heller School, the Long Island Jewish Medical Center, and the Franklin and Eleanor Roosevelt Institute.
1988...Honored by the World Rehabilitation Fund and the New York Consumer Assembly.
1989...Elected President of JJCC.
1990...Elected President and CEO of JJCC.

Sol Chick Chaikin married Rosalind Bryon on August 31, 1940. His extended family included seven children and twelve grandchildren. In retirement he said his greatest pleasures were the hours he could spend with his wife, daughter, sons, daughters-in-law, grandchildren, and friends.

He died on April 1, 1991 of heart failure.

# *Bibliography*

Allen, Louis, *Burma The Longest War*. (New York: St. Martins Press), 1984.

Chaikin, Sol Chick, *A Labor Viewpoint: Another Opinion*. (Monroe, New York: Library Research Associates Inc.), 1980.

*The Chaikin Presidency*, Cornell Unviersity, Martin P. Catherwood Library, Labor-Management Documentation Center, ILGWU Archives .

Cohen, Herbert J., ed., *Page One: Major Events 1920-1981. As presented in the New York Times*. ( New York: Arno Press), 1981

*Current Biography*, (April 1979).

Fischer, Edward, *The Chancy War*. (New York: Orion Books), 1991

*Juris Doctor*, ( Jan. 1978).

Martin, John G., DVM, *It Began At Imphal The Combat Cargo Story*. (Manhattan, Kansas: Sunflower University Press), 1988

Maurer Maurer, Editor, *Combat Squadrons of the Air Force, World War II*. (Albert F. Simpson Historical Research Center and Office of Air Force History, Headquarters USAF), 1982

McCollough, David, *Truman*, (New York: Simon and Shuster), 1992

*The New York Times Index, A Book of Record 1945*

*The Times in Review, 1940-1949*, (New York: Arno Press)

# Acknowledgments

I am indebted more than I can say:

To my grandson M. Reed Chaikin who introduced me to the computer, started me on WORD, and remained on call day and night until I learned to love it — and then more.

To Phil Comstock and Maier Fox for their initial research that made my journey through this book possible.

To my daughter Karen Chaikin who cried and laughed along the way, and gave me the heart to keep going. To my children Eric, Stacey, David, Wendy, Robert and Marilyn, for their confidence in my effort.

To Rochelle Natt, a dynamic poet, who introduced me to the outstanding novelist Caroline Leavitt who knew all the right questions to ask.

To Bertha Hartman for her careful readings, her valuable comments, and for her constant support and friendship in the face of endless revisions.

To Ruth Englander who was there, with her finely tuned ear and sensitive spirit, from my very first musings to the completion of this work.

To Ethel Romm and Kent Ozarow for their reading, editing, and caring about words with just the right meaning.

To my cousins Larry and Saul Hofstein who scoured their own trove of treasures to find World War II letters for me.

To Delia Gottlieb for being there, and to Caroline Zainer, Jean Young, Phyllis Brusiloff, and Jean De Mesquita for their encouragement and enthusiasm.

To Rabbi Robert S. Widom, for his steadfast support over these many years.

And with very special thanks to Lou Dorfsman who freely offered his invaluable friendship, time, skill, and discerning eye when it counted.

Rosalind Bryon Chaikin

# Index

# ABOUT THE AUTHOR

Rosalind Bryon Chaikin has devoted much of her life to family and children, beginning with her own children, grandchildren, and now great-grandchildren. She began her career in a special education program designed to allow blind children to live at home with their families and attend their neighborhood schools. Her teaching skills soon included visually impaired along with learning disabled from kindergarten through twelfth grade. As a member of a special resource team she participated in curriculum development and gave in-service teacher training classes.

Once retired, she served on the Boards of the National Jewish Hospital/National Asthma Center in Denver, the National Council of Jewish Women/New York Section, and the Child Care Action Campaign. She is currently an active board member of the Mental Health Association in Nassau County, the Board of Overseers of the Florence Heller School of Advanced Studies in Social Welfare at Brandeis University, and the chair of the Advisory Board for the Family and Children's Policy Center at the Heller School.

She has written several articles on analytical thinking and co-authored a manual on visual performance. Together with author Ethel Romm, she co-edited *A Labor Viewpoint/Another Opinion* by Sol Chick Chaikin, published in 1980.

Widowed after 51 years of marriage, and inspired by her husband's wartime letters, she has moved into the world of poetry and prose. Her poems of love, loss and laughter have been well received among young and old alike. This frank and loving memoir is her first book.